Public Access:

Citizens and
Collective Bargaining
in the Public Schools

Robert E. Doherty
editor

Papers from the symposium Citizen Participation in
the Collective Bargaining Process in Public Education
at the New York State School of Industrial and Labor
Relations, Cornell University, Ithaca, New York
October 2 and 3, 1978

New York State
School of Industrial and
Labor Relations
Cornell University
1979

Cover design by Lynda A. Schulz
Cover photograph by Rondal Partridge

Library of Congress Catalog Card Number: 79-13189
International Standard Book Number: 0-87546-073-9

Copies of this book can be ordered from
ILR Publications Division
New York State School of Industrial and Labor Relations
Cornell University, Box 1000
Ithaca, New York 14853

Library of Congress Cataloging in Publication Data
Main entry under title:

Public access.

   "Papers from the symposium Citizen Participation in the
Collective Bargaining Process in Public Education, New
York State School of Industrial and Labor Relations,
Cornell University, Ithaca, New York, October 2 and 3,
1978.
   1. Collective bargaining—Teachers—United States—
Congresses. I. Doherty, Robert Emmett, 1923-
II. Cornell University. New York State School of Indus-
trial and Labor Relations.
LB2842.2.P82   331.89'041'371100973   79-13189
ISBN 0-87546-073-9

Contents

v Introduction

viii Participants

I.
1 On the Merits of Greater
Public Access to the
Bargaining Process:
An Equivocal View
Robert E. Doherty

8 Response
*Comment by
Harold R. Newman
Discussion Highlights*

II.
14 The Public Access Movement
in California
Ralph J. Flynn

21 Response
*Comment by Kurt Hanslowe
Discussion Highlights*

III.
29 The Basis for a New Parent-
Teacher Relationship in
Collective Bargaining
David S. Seeley

39 Sunshine Bargaining:
The Case for Public
Participation
Donald Magruder

46 Response
*Comment by
Ronald Donovan
Discussion Highlights*

IV.
54 Parent Participation in
Collective Bargaining:
Rochester, New York
Gayle Dixon

V.
63 A Teacher Perspective on
School Governance and
Collective Bargaining
John E. Dunlop

74 Citizen Involvement in
Teacher Negotiations:
A Caution
Robert P. Bates

78 Response
*Comment by
Mary McCormick
Discussion Highlights*

VI.
87 The Parents' Role in
Collective Bargaining
Happy Craven Fernandez

95 Response
*Comment by
Edward B. Krinsky
Discussion Highlights*

Introduction

This is a volume filled with opinions. There are some facts here and there and a modicum of analysis, but mainly what the reader will find are opinions. That was the plan. Until recently, concern about the public achieving greater influence on bargaining processes and outcomes in the schools has been so slight that gathering data on the subject is next to impossible; any attempt at systematic analysis would be an exercise in folly.

The purpose behind the symposium was to bring together the main actors in what may turn out to be act one, scene one, of an interesting drama. Those actors were teacher organization leaders, public school officials, labor relations neutrals, and representatives of public interest groups primarily concerned about the conduct of public education.

There were also three academic contributors, but they were stand-ins for individuals who announced almost at the last minute that they could not attend. This is not said to derogate the contributions of the professors but to point up the purpose of the symposium. It was intended to serve as a forum for those with a stake in the collective bargaining process and who also, we suspected, had some rather strong notions about the appropriateness of providing more direct public access to that process. Before long, academics will apply their finely honed analytical tools to the matter, explaining why it failed or why it flourished, depending on the way things turn out. Those ventures will be all to the good. We did not think that the time and place for that sort of endeavor was Ithaca, New York, in October of 1978. Mostly we were interested in hearing what was on the minds of those who had given thought to the matter and who represented substantial constituencies. Their papers were not presented in any special order. If there was any guiding principle in determining program format it was that of accommodating the travel plans of the participants.

Public access to the bargaining process is a phrase that is both infelicitous and ambiguous. Lacking the wit to make it more felicitous, I shall concentrate on the ambiguity. What that phrase has come to mean is a method whereby the public (or various publics) has an opportunity to influence the outcome of the bargaining. Public access can take several forms. Sunshine bargaining, as provided for in the Florida collective bargaining statute, is a type of public access since the assumption behind that legislation is that the parties will behave differently when they bargain in public view than they would if they bargained behind closed doors. The provision in the California statute that states that union and management contract proposals must be published well before talks begin and that these proposals may be discussed in an open forum is a form of public access. Similarly, the procedure in Wisconsin allows for public discussion of union and management proposals before bargaining begins. The formation of a parents' union, as described in Happy Fernandez's paper, is a dramatic type of public access. Perhaps the most direct form of public access is the technique used in Rochester, New York, described in Gayle Dixon's paper. There a "citizen" representative served on the school board's bargaining team. Another scheme that has been proposed but rarely implemented is a public referendum on the contract before it can be implemented.

All these techniques seem to have their origin in a growing sense of unease about bargaining in the public schools, in gnawing doubts about whether school officials and teacher unions left to their own devices can come up with a settlement that will contain any benefits for school children. As it is pointed out in a number of papers, there appears to have been a decline in student achievement in recent years, accompanied by a substantial increase in per student costs and a decline in public confidence in the schools. Many see bargaining as one of the important causes of this mischief, and one of the reasons bargaining has contributed to these problems is that the parties to the bargain are insulated from public scrutiny and influence.

Teacher organization representatives, of course, take a different view of the matter. They argue that the public's view is heard through its representation on the school board, which bears final responsibility for the settlement. They also point out that the trades and compromises essential to bringing bargaining to a conclusion would not be possible if both the public and rank-and-file teachers were constantly looking over the bargainers' shoulders.

Portions of the discussion following each presentation have been included in this volume because in many instances these clarified some murky points made in the papers and gave the author an opportunity to elaborate on particular themes. One issue that was only implied in the papers but became clear in the discussion was that "access" advocates were less concerned about the form public access ought to take than they were about the public being kept in the dark about what transpired at the bargaining table.

As in most endeavors of this kind, very few, if any, participants found the arguments of those holding opposing views persuasive. Those holding strong views on any side of the issue did, however, discover that those holding opposing positions could be reasonable people with legitimate interests to advance and protect. Out of such exchanges, we are told, emerges the beginning of wisdom.

Robert E. Doherty
Associate Dean
New York State School
of Industrial and Labor Relations
Cornell University

Participants

Ellen Ainsworth is codirector of the Information Project on Educational Negotiations, which is conducted by the Institute for Responsive Education. She has acted as a consultant on school finance and collective bargaining to the League of Women Voters of California, and she is a coauthor, with Jackie Berman and Charles Cheng, of *You, the Schools, and Collective Bargaining*, a handbook for citizens.

Douglas J.Bantle is a specialist in public sector labor relations in the Rochester office of the New York State School of Industrial and Labor Relations of Cornell University. A past member of the New York State United Teachers, the Fairport Central School District Board of Education, and the New York State School Boards Association, he now serves on mediation and factfinding panels for the New York State Public Employment Relations Board.

Robert P. Bates has been affiliated with the American Federation of Teachers since 1967. At present, he is director of field services for that organization, with responsibilities for the negotiation of numerous big-city collective agreements. Earlier in his career he was, successively, a classroom teacher, president of a teachers' union local, and director of the Wisconsin Federation of Teachers.

Gayle Dixon is the parent representative to the Rochester school district negotiating team. She is president of a local PTA unit and is a member of Parent Leadership, an advisory council to Rochester's board of education.

Robert E. Doherty, associate dean of the New York State School of Industrial and Labor Relations, is a mediator, fact finder, and arbitrator in public sector disputes. He has initiated programs to train neutrals and has evaluated a number of neutral agencies. His writings on public sector employment include *Teachers, School Boards, and Collective Bargaining: A Changing of the Guard,* of which he is coauthor with Walter Oberer.

Ronald Donovan, since 1955 a professor in the New York State School of Industrial and Labor Relations at Cornell University, frequently serves as a mediator and fact finder in public sector labor disputes. He teaches a course in public sector bargaining and trains union and management advocates for work in the public sector.

John Dunlop is manager of the National Education Association's office of negotiations. Before assuming his present responsibilities, he was a negotiations specialist and field representative for the association and chief negotiator for the Hawaii State Teachers Association. A member of the District of Columbia Bar, he began his career in education as a secondary school classroom teacher.

Happy Craven Fernandez is cochairperson of Parents' Union for Public Schools in Philadelphia, an independent parents' organization that focuses on such city-wide issues as collective bargaining, desegregation, and parents' rights. She was a founder of the Powelton-Mantua Children's School, a public, parent-initiated open education school and the Powelton-Mantua Educational Fund, a neighborhood-based education advocacy organization, and is the author of the handbook *Parents Organizing to Improve Schools.* In addition to her volunteer work, she is an assistant professor in the School of Social Administration at Temple University.

Ralph J. Flynn, state executive director of the California Teachers Association, has long experience in public employee organizations. A past executive director of the Coalition of American Public Employees, he has also been an executive in the National Education Association responsible for affiliate services and a teacher's assistance fund. He is the author of *Public Work, Public Workers.*

Kurt L. Hanslowe, a professor in the Cornell Law School and the New York State School of Industrial and Labor Relations at Cornell University, is a consultant to New York's state law revision commission and the New York State Public Employment Relations Board. A former assistant general counsel to the United Automobile Workers, he is now active as an arbitrator of grievance disputes in both the public and private sectors. He is the author of *The Emerging Law of Labor Relations in Public Employment* and a coauthor of *The Taylor Act: A Primer for School Personnel and Other Beginners at Collective Negotiations.*

Robert D. Helsby is director of Public Employment Relations Services, a national project, sponsored by the Carnegie Corporation, to increase the efficiency and competency of public employment labor relations boards. He came to his present position after serving as chairman of the New

York State Public Employment Relations Board from 1967 to 1977. Earlier, he was dean for continuing education at the State University of New York and executive deputy industrial commissioner of the New York State Department of Labor.

Francine Herman, associate professor in the School of Hotel Administration at Cornell University, specializes in labor-management relations and communications and often teaches in the extension programs offered by Cornell's New York State School of Industrial and Labor Relations. She recently served as chairwoman of a U.S. Department of Labor advisory committee to review mine health and safety training program regulations and has been a mediator and fact finder for the New York State Public Employment Relations Board since 1970.

Edward B. Krinsky is associate director of employment relations studies at the Wisconsin Center for Public Policy. Now an independent labor arbitrator, he previously served as a mediator and arbitrator for the Wisconsin Employment Relations Commission and taught industrial relations at the University of Wisconsin, Madison. Among his writings for journals in the field is "Public Access to Public Sector Collective Bargaining in Wisconsin."

Vito Longo has worked as a teacher, administrator, and negotiator for the public schools. Since 1970 he has been with the New York State Education Department. At present he is supervisor of educational employment relations in that department and serves as a consultant to the department's commission on public employment relations and to local school districts.

Mary McCormick is an adjunct professor at the Graduate School of Business at Columbia University whose academic interests are in the area of public sector management and labor relations. She has served as a special assistant to New York's deputy mayor for labor relations and as research director for the temporary commission on New York City finances.

Robert B. McKersie is dean of the New York State School of Industrial and Labor Relations at Cornell University and a professor in the school. Before coming to Cornell, he taught at the University of Chicago. He has acted as a consultant to numerous public and private sector organizations, including the National Commission on Productivity, and has been a member of the president's advisory committee on federal pay, the educational panel of the American Arbitration Association, the New York State Mediation Board, and the New York State Public Employment Relations Board.

Donald Magruder, executive director of the Florida School Boards Association, lectures frequently on the subject of sunshine bargaining. A former high school teacher, he has been director of noninstructional personnel, executive assistant superintendent for personnel relations, and chief negotiator for a local school district in Florida. He is the founder of the Florida School Labor Relations Service and the author of *Bargaining in Public: Help or Hindrance?*

Harold R. Newman has been chairman of the New York State Public Employment Relations Board since 1977 and previously served as director of the board's conciliation office, where he was responsible for impasse resolution in New York's public sector. A frequent lecturer in the labor relations field, he has, in addition to his experience as a neutral, worked for public and private sector unions and acted as a management consultant in labor and public relations problems.

John A. Ryan, the chief negotiator for the Philadelphia Federation of Teachers, is a vice president of the American Federation of Teachers and a frequent participant in the national functions of the AFL-CIO. On leave from his position as head of a high school social studies department, he is active in the Phi Delta Kappa professional fraternity for educators.

David Seeley is director of the Public Education Association, an independent citizens' organization concerned with the quality of public education. Previously, he was the Mayor's Office of Education liaison with the Human Resources Administration; in the U.S. Office of Education he was assistant commissioner for equal educational opportunity and special assistant to the U.S. commissioner of education; and in the U.S. Department of Health, Education, and Welfare, he served as attorney in the office of the general counsel.

Eris Thompson, president of the New York State Congress of Parents and Teachers, has recently initiated that organization's study of collective bargaining in the New York State public schools. She is an officer of the New York State Educational Conference Board, a group concerned with school finance and state legislation affecting public schools, and she is a member of the state's Special Task Force on Equity and Excellence in Education.

I.

On the Merits of Greater Public Access to the Bargaining Process: An Equivocal View

Robert E. Doherty

It is probably no exaggeration to say that most citizens nowadays view the governmental process with suspicion and government performance with disappointment. One of the most frequently heard complaints is that the regulatory agencies have been captured by the regulated and that traditional adversaries have become collusive partners. And all the while, the public is having unseemly things done to it.

Now a movement is afoot to do something about the governmental process. Although we have not yet complied with Woodrow Wilson's injunction of "open convenants openly arrived at," there is a stirring about to open things up in federal, state, and local governments. In many instances, regulatory and administrative agencies now must conduct their meetings under public view, the hope being that there will be far less hanky-panky under this arrangement than prevailed before.

Whether all this "sunshine" will cause a new growth of public trust on the one hand and greater government responsiveness on the other is an open question. Skeptics will continue to believe that as long as there is sufficient incentive to cut deals in the shadows no amount of public zeal and scrutiny will prevent that from happening. It is also at least arguable that in some circumstances, labor relations being a case in point, progress cannot be made, settlements cannot be reached, unless the advocate decision makers have an opportunity to meet covertly from time to time in order to write the script that will make the fait accompli more palatable to the various constituencies.

As for performance, who has not heard criticism of, or themselves criticized, the performance of government agencies? Right now it is a quasi-public agency, the U.S. Postal Service, that appears to be receiving the greatest amount of public animus. But there are other contenders, and certainly near the head of the pack are the public schools. There is a growing number of individuals who believe that opening up the decision-making process will not only ensure more responsiveness and less chicanery, it will make our public institutions better, or, to use a phrase much in currency these days, more cost-effective.

The interest in more direct citizen participation in the bargaining process is, I think, a part of this larger concern about government agencies. What distinguishes those who seek greater access to decision making in the schools is that rather than being frustrated by an often indifferent, frequently incompetent, perhaps sometimes venal bureaucracy, they feel thwarted by something called collective bargaining. Another difference—and that is why we are discussing these issues today—is that they have a specific objective in mind, and they have some notions as to how to go about achieving it.

Now it is easy to romanticize about the good old days when school boards were presumably the embodiment of the public will and always responsive to the needs of citizens, children, and taxpayers, while simultaneously treating teachers with fairness and generosity. That is not a very accurate picture. It is also easy to exaggerate the coercive power of unions. "Would that we had half the power attributed to us" is a constant union leader plaint. Yet if collective bargaining really works, if public officials agree to do things they would rather not do (indeed, agree to do things they think they *ought* not do) because of the pressures engendered by bargaining, then they become by that degree less responsive to their constituents. I leave aside for the moment a consideration of whether bilateral decisions reached through bargaining are inferior or superior to decisions reached when school boards enjoyed more unilateral authority. It is the process value of representative government that is at issue here—how ought critical decisions affecting the conduct of a public enterprise be made?—not whether one mechanism produces better results than the other.

In most school districts voters elect board members who in turn appoint administrators who are responsible for carrying out the bargaining. Thus, superficially viewed, there is accountability. Administrators can be fired and board members turned out of office if the bargaining does not go well. And if these measures do not work, we can, in most jurisdictions, deny the culprits the wherewithal to carry out their nefarious schemes by voting down the budget. That ought to be all the accountability one could ask for in a democratic society.

Be that as it may, there seems to be something about collective bargaining that prevents the democratic process from working quite that smoothly. Public influence does get blunted along the way; public officials do agree to things that the majority of citizens, if given a choice, would probably not approve. This happens, I think, because of the peculiar nature of the bargaining process. Of all interest groups concerned about policy and the allocation of resources, the union has the most privileged position. Board representatives are required by law to (eventually) make a deal with it in the form of a collective bargaining contract. Other claimants can be consulted and listened to, but these groups have no authority to force a deal in quite the manner the union does.

It is this need to come up with a settlement, to make a deal with the union, that tends to insulate the employer from whatever pressures may be emanating from these other claimants. One is disposed to listen more attentively to the party who has the capacity to do one mischief than to the party who merely states claims, no matter how highly principled these claims might be.

A citizen group might object, for example, to a union proposal to base the right of teacher transfer entirely on seniority, its position being that the right to assign teachers to particular schools is a management prerogative and should therefore be controlled through the political process. The reason behind the objection might be the fear that the inner city schools would be forever staffed by fledgling teachers, all of them waiting to build up enough seniority to permit them to move on. Now assume the union feels keenly about the transfer proposal. It is not difficult to understand why teachers should want such a provision. Suppose they feel keenly enough to make substantial economic concessions to get it or threaten a strike. What countermeasures are available to our group of citizens? How does the system accommodate their interests? It does not, and it probably cannot. In most instances, the decision will be made behind closed doors; the public will find out about it when the contract is summarized in the daily paper.

As was suggested earlier, those who advocate greater citizen participation in the collective bargaining process seem also to be persuaded that their participation will improve the quality of the schools. That might or might not happen. It is possible to have good schools that are bureaucratically controlled, and it is possible to have poor ones that are models of democracy. Democracy is no more a guarantee of quality than authoritarian control is of mediocrity.

Still, the performance of the schools, at least as can be measured by student achievement tests, has declined substantially in recent years. And because that decline has coincided with the growth of bargaining, many citizens see a causal connection. (We shall have more to say about the possibility of such a connection later.) But whether there is something about bargaining that affects student achievement or not, the decline in test scores is real. Median Standard Achievement Test (SAT) scores declined steadily from 1966 to 1974, from a median verbal score of approximately 460 to 440. Median math scores dropped from 497 to 480 during the same period. There have been similar though not quite so dramatic declines in other measurements as well: American College Testing, Minnesota Scholastic Aptitude, and the Iowa Test of Educational Development, for example. The U.S. government–sponsored National Assessment of Educational Progress of 1976 showed the same dreary results.

Clearly something is wrong, and it is just as clear that the reason cannot be because we have shortchanged the schools financially. During the period the SAT scores were declining, per pupil costs as a percentage of per capita disposable income rose from 23 to 29 percent; the portion of the gross national product spent on public education rose from 2.8 to 3.6 percent.

Now the point must be made that these figures on both performance and cost are aggregate figures and include both organized and unorganized districts. We do not know whether students in districts where teachers are organized perform better or worse or cost more or less to educate than students in systems that are not organized but are otherwise similar. It is sufficient for many only to believe there is a connection between bargaining on the one hand and declining performance and increasing costs on the other. *Post hoc ergo propter hoc.*

Before we could assume that public participation will reverse the decline in student performance it would have to be demonstrated that there are provisions in collective bargaining agreements, provisions that became a part of personnel policy only because of the coercive power of the union, that are harmful to educational quality. Teacher transfer rights have already been mentioned as an example of a "harmful" personnel policy that owes its existence to collective bargaining. Most teachers would probably rather not teach in schools highly populated with disadvantaged children. Many would like some assurance that after having served their apprenticeship in the disadvantaged schools they could bid successfully for an opportunity to teach in happier surroundings. Thus there is pressure on union leadership to push hard for contract language that makes seniority the primary criterion for transfer. Parents whose children study under this "revolving door" policy object. They want their children to learn under more experienced teachers. Few seem to find it persuasive that, according to a recent production function study of the Philadelphia schools,[1] disadvantaged students tend to

---

1. Anita A. Summers and Barbara L. Wolfe, "Which School Resources Help Learning? Efficiency and Equity in Philadelphia Public Schools," *Business Review* (Federal Reserve Bank of Philadelphia), February 1975, pp. 4–29.

perform slightly better under inexperienced teachers than they do when exposed to teachers with long seniority.

This example of a group of teachers pursuing their own interests does not suggest, of course, that union demands are always, or usually, *designed* to promote the interests of children. It does suggest, however, that on occasion the pursuit of narrow interests can have laudable results. Teachers sometimes really do want what students need. It would be more difficult to make a case that union proposals on job security benefit school children. (I speak here of so-called fair dismissal or just cause provisions that would give to probationary teachers a degree of security equal to or superior to the security enjoyed by tenured teachers.) Broadly construed, these provisions would, for all practical purposes, eliminate the probationary period and make it almost impossible for a district to dismiss a teacher absent proof of gross incompetence or wrongdoing.

Similarly, it is not easy to see how a generous personal leave policy for teachers improves the learning environment. It is not uncommon for teachers in New York State to have three or four days of such paid leave each year—no questions asked. To the extent teachers take advantage of this provision, students will spend more time with caretaker substitutes while spending less time with regular teachers. If one can make the assumption that very little instruction goes on under a substitute teacher and if one further assumes that a substantial portion of authorized leave days are in fact taken, it follows that this is one union demand that cannot be justified on the grounds that it is good for kids. It is no easier to justify contract provisions that reduce the number of student-teacher contact hours by shortening the school year or that require that classes be dismissed early so that such duties as grading report cards and consulting with parents, duties that used to be performed after school, can be performed during the regular school day. It is worth noting in the context of these provisions that one of the more persuasive explanations for the dramatic decline in test scores in recent years is the equally dramatic decline in the number of hours students spend in classroom instruction. In Fairfield, Connecticut, to use a district that might be representative, annual contact hours declined from one thousand in 1955 to nine hundred in 1975.[2] To be sure, much of the reduction in time spent in academic work over the last two decades cannot be attributed to collective bargaining, but just as surely some of it can.

Although it is difficult to demonstrate that many contractual provisions promote student learning, it may be possible to justify them

---

2. Edward B. Fiske, "Study Finds School Children Now Getting Less Instruction," *New York Times*, 4 May 1977, p. 50.

on the ground that they are good for teachers. It is important that we do not lose sight of the fact—the rhetoric of statutory preambles to the contrary notwithstanding—that the purpose behind collective bargaining statutes, from the Wagner Act to the most recent teacher collective negotiations law, is not to improve the quality of any given enterprise but to provide basic rights for employees. Albert Shanker put it as well as anybody can when he observed

It's possible in the bargaining process to negotiate things that are good for children, and it's possible to negotiate things that are bad for children. The chances are that most things that are negotiated don't have much to do with children at all. They have to do with whether teachers are going to feel happy about their jobs and whether they're going to have a better standard of living.[3]

That is why we have collective bargaining legislation, to give legal support to the notion that more benefits will be forthcoming if workers stand together than if they stand separately.

To put the issue perhaps too baldly, it may be too much to expect an employee organization that is legally and perhaps morally bound to advance the interests of those it represents to subordinate that obligation in the interest of promoting the welfare of a school district. We do not make similar demands of the United Auto Workers in its dealings with General Motors, and one might question whether we ought to ask more of the American Federation of Teachers or the National Education Association than we do of any other union. It is the employer's responsibility to promote the enterprise's welfare; one of the ways to do that is to resist union incursions in those areas that may jeopardize efficiency and quality.

Even though it is difficult to disentangle the consequences of bargaining from the influences of other factors, the evidence is pretty clear that bargaining does work. Teachers do seem to enjoy somewhat higher salaries and greater benefits under bargaining than they would have without it. Even in those districts where teachers do not bargain, benefits seem to have spilled over from districts that do. Perhaps the best evidence that bargaining works to teachers' advantage is the enthusiasm with which teachers take to it. They have been most energetic in lobbying for enabling legislation, and once these bills are passed, they join unions in droves. It is not likely that we would see all that voluntary activity if the dues money did not buy something.

Now the question of whether collective bargaining is sometimes too successful is raised. A number of citizen and parent organizations seem to be saying that it is not possible to continue to accommodate teacher interests without threatening the welfare of the educational enterprise.

---

3. *Chicago Tribune*, 7 March 1977, p. 4.

Bargaining, it is alleged, has caused school boards to be less accountable and has probably contributed to the decline in student performance as well. The goal of fair treatment for teachers, which bargaining presumably affords, and the at least equally laudable goals of public responsiveness and high student achievement are irreconcilable.

If we cannot have it both ways, this argument continues, then our energies ought to be directed at the much more important mission of seeing to it that the schools are run democratically and efficiently. If bargaining suffers and teachers come to enjoy fewer rights and privileges as a result, so be it. The tail has wagged the dog long enough.

Is it possible to have collective bargaining without doing mischief to the broader social goals of accountability and high educational achievement? I would like to believe that it is. We are not likely to return to the prebargaining era. Collective bargaining is a valued process that has had overwhelming legislative approval; but equally firm is the public's belief that the basic direction of our public institutions ought to be determined by the people who pay for them and depend upon the benefits these institutions confer. There is a conflict of laudable goals.

The trick is to figure out a way of reducing this conflict in a manner that will allow for more direct public participation in the bargaining process without unduly frustrating the genuine aspirations of teachers. I do not have the wit to devise a scheme for doing that. But I am heartened to learn that there are those here who do.

Response

Comment by Harold R. Newman

I think it was Saint Paul who said in a peevish moment, "Because thou blowest neither hot nor cold I spew thee out of my mouth." But I am not really irritated with Bob Doherty's equivocation on greater public access. In some measure, I share it. I am not élitist enough to tell the public that any governmental process is none of their business. Governmental process is their business. I am much troubled, however, because almost ten years as a professional mediator and almost thirty years total experience with public and private sector labor relations have caused me to believe that labor negotiation is not a process that lends itself to public viewing without grievous injury to the process as well as to the negotiators.

Bob Doherty suggests that, at least superficially, there may be accountability in school district bargaining because school boards are elected by the voters and these boards in turn appoint administrators who are responsible for carrying out the bargaining. My own experience, at least that of recent years, tells me that while administrators may be part of the school district's bargaining team, it is a professional management advocate, usually with substantial private sector experience, who serves as the board's chief negotiator. School boards in our state and elsewhere have learned that, with employee wages and fringes making up a substantial part of the total school district budget, collective negotiations are too important to be left to the amateur or the tyro. Management's chief negotiator is likely to be as unhappy as his or her union counterpart with a demand to bargain in the sunshine. A professional negotiator is likely to view public access to bargaining as at least a nuisance and perhaps a serious impediment to settlement.

I suppose I really part company with Bob Doherty when he suggests that since school boards are required by law to deal with unions, the board has to listen "more attentively to the party who has the capacity to do one mischief than to the party who merely states claims, no matter how highly principled these claims might be."

For the past few years, at least in New York State, I have seen no evidence of boards of education acting as though they are feeling great pressure from the unions representing professional, blue-collar, and white-collar employees. As I write, there is a strike of teachers in the Long Island area, which has been in effect for three weeks. When the teachers struck, they had no demands on the bargaining table. The board had fifteen. Among these fifteen were proposals for a two-year wage freeze (in a district without an increment structure for faculty), abolition of a dental plan, abolition of a teacher welfare fund, and removal of a contract clause that involved job security. The wreckage of teacher salary schedules containing indexes, the reduction of sabbaticals, wage freezes, and abolition of fringe benefits of every kind have been strewn over the bargaining sea these past few years. Even without much public access to negotiations, the boards of education have listened to the voices of the Jarvisites with far more attention than to the crisis threats of the unionists.

I share Bob Doherty's concerns about the dwindling scores in student achievement tests, but I have seen no solid evidence offered by anyone that this is caused by teachers' collective bargaining. I suspect it has much to do with present American values, TV culture, and national priorities. If, however, teachers have won demands in bargaining that hinder the learning process for students, there has been a failure not only of the boards of education that agreed to such demands but of neutral agencies like mine, which did not perhaps make these demands nonmandatory or indeed prohibited subjects of bargaining.

It is high fashion now to urge public access to all types of government process. New York Secretary of State Mario Cuomo, who does not to my knowledge pander to what is simply popular, has been critical of certain public bodies throughout the state that seek to circumvent the open meetings law by "designating their gatherings as 'informal' or as 'workshops,' 'work sessions,' 'study sessions,' and the like." Apparently, there is some problem even with government agencies not involved in labor relations in providing public access. Strong advocates of sunshine laws might take note, however, of the recent decision of the Iowa Supreme Court exempting contract negotiations from that state's sunshine law; the court cited two other cases, one in New Hampshire and one in Nevada, in support of its own decision.

We know that a sophisticated union bargaining team in the public or private sector will come to the table asking far more than it expects to get in economic and noneconomic concessions. We know that sophisticated bargainers for management in both sectors will be far more conservative at the outset of negotiations than they expect they will have to be later on to get a settlement. There is no lack of honesty in this approach. They both understand that if they start from their bottom line they have no place to go. Will those given public access to the bargaining understand this ballet? Or will they cry out against the outrageous demands of the teachers or perhaps the outrageous rigidity of the board's negotiators? I am afraid that they might indeed do one or the other. What opportunity is there in the sunshine for the bargainers to feel and probe each other's positions to determine which are "hard" and which are "soft" and what can be traded for what? This is why I am a little less equivocal than Bob Doherty: I think we need more public access to the bargaining process, but not at the table. I think we need some trust that the taxpayers and parents are well represented by boards of educations. I truly believe they are.

There is yet another question, one that goes to the heart of the matter: Who is the public? There are clearly many publics, each with separate and often lamentably narrow interests. In their study *The Public Interest in Government Labor Relations*, Jean J. Couturier and Richard Schick found that, while there is a perceived public interest in public sector bargaining, usually only private or special interests present themselves. Couturier and Schick propose that there should be means for public access to and influence on bargaining short of direct participation.[1] Few would disagree that there is a public interest to be attended to and that it is necessary to experiment with procedures for access short of direct participation in the bargaining. All of public sector labor negotiations is so new that it may be considered to be in the laboratory stage, even in states with statutes as old as those in Wisconsin, Michigan, and New York. Indeed, the variety of statutes across the country provides for experimentation in all areas of public sector collective bargaining, and experimental procedures to provide public access without involvement at the bargaining table are imperative.

Discussion Highlights

In discussion following the Doherty and Newman presentations, the conference participants considered public frustrations with school governance and addressed the problem of whether school boards adequately represent the public. They debated how to identify other representatives

1. Jean J. Couturier and Richard Schick, *The Public Interest in Government Labor Relations* (Cambridge, Mass.: Ballinger Publishing Co., 1977).

of the public and whether these representatives should be present at the bargaining table—*Editor.*

David Seeley (Public Education Association): Harold, I wonder if I could at least raise a little question in your mind with regard to some of the violent manifestations you have attributed to the public access movement. Would you be willing to consider the possibility that these ugly manifestations come not because of public access but because of the lack of it? That this is frustration people are expressing because there isn't any good vehicle to represent their interest?

Harold Newman (New York State Public Employment Relations Board): David, let me confess that that has occurred to me. In fact, it has occurred to me more than once, that this kind of irrational behavior which occurs from time to time may in fact result from a kind of frustration with not being able to have an input. People who don't have a chance to express themselves end up expressing themselves irrationally. But I also believe, along with Couturier and Schick, whose book I made reference to, that there is no homogeneous group called "the public."

Kurt Hanslowe (Cornell University): Harold, I'm mildly perplexed by one thing: why would it be so catastrophically disastrous to have one or two spokesmen for some public or other make their pitches at a factfinding proceeding? Why must they be excluded if they want to have a say? The fact finder may conclude afterwards that their presentation was a lot of nonsense and he isn't going to pay any attention to it—why do they have to be kept out of it?

Harold Newman: I could be a wise guy and say that the reason is that my budget won't permit me to have these extended factfinding appearances, but that obviously is not it. The reason is that I am very fearful about becoming a little bit pregnant. If we turn the factfinding process into a public hearing, which I don't think the statute anticipates, we open the door to all sorts of interest groups. If we follow that proposal, I'm not going to know from whence cometh all of the people who identify themselves as being parties in interest—and this isn't simply a matter of fussy administrative concerns.

Robert McKersie (Cornell University): But Harold, there are no absolutes. I would agree that if you stay with what collective bargaining requires as a process, these requirements lead you very directly to the conclusion that discussions have got to be off the record. But collective bargaining is not a preeminent institution. There are other values, other forces. Indeed, even in the private sector (where we say there aren't as many contending challenges), if collective bargaining brings us to a national emergency dispute, we do some things that are not natural to collective bargaining. The absolute of saying "Let collective bargaining do what it has to do to get the job done" has to be laid alongside what other people here are saying—namely, there are other institutions, other groups.

It is a power situation. Knowledge is power, and a lot of people don't have the knowledge they need to participate. It is not a question of just closing the door on access. We have to get into a hardheaded discussion about the era we are in, the circumstances and procedures around which access can take place. It is going to be messy. Bargaining is messy. We have to come up with some bigger views of decision making in the public sector than what is afforded us by just following the dictates of collective bargaining.

Harold Newman: I once wrote an article saying that every time the question of public access is brought up, I get bitten—because the people are a great beast. In this period of Proposition 13 this is an odd thing to say, but I think government does a much better and a more conscientious job than most people believe, and I think that school boards and school superintendents do a much more honest job of representing management than is perceived by the outraged taxpayer. But I certainly did not intend by anything I said to close the door. Quite the opposite. I wish we had found the means. I just throw up my hands and say I don't know what it is at this point.

Ellen Ainsworth (Information Project on Educational Negotiations): I am puzzled by your earlier statement, Harold. There seems to me an underlying assumption that the public cannot understand this process, and if they cannot understand it, it is easier to leave them out. There *are* a great many publics, but most of them do indeed understand the ballet dance. I think it is a mistake to assume that people cannot understand the governmental process.

Donald Magruder (Florida School Boards Association): I would like to ask you a question, Harold. Who represents the public in the election of officials who run our government?

Harold Newman: As you know, Don, when you get into office after having run on a platform, there is a difference between what you philosophically believe and what you discover after you get there. I think the best we can ask from representative government is that the guy do an honest job. The only way I can answer your question is to say that if representatives do represent the public that elects them and if the public doesn't like what they have done, the public has the ability to vote them out of office. This certainly goes for school board members.

Donald Magruder: How about for the collective bargaining contract?

Harold Newman: The buck stops with the school board. We have, time after time, seen the public defeat budgets: sometimes, I think, because of public irritation with what is happening with collective bargaining; other times because of a general irritation—they feel that they are being overtaxed; sometimes, I'm afraid, because they don't have any particular commitment to schools and to education. It is interesting to note that in the states that don't have any collective bargaining law for teachers, like Ohio and Illinois, they have more teacher strikes than New York, and we have a much larger number of school districts. This is because people simply vote not to increase the millage and give the schools the money with which to run. The problem lies much deeper than the whole question of collective bargaining.

II.

The Public Access Movement in California

Ralph J. Flynn

The purpose of this symposium is to assess the impact of collective bargaining on the public's access to the educational enterprise. The obvious concern is that through the collective bargaining process teachers may remove from the public domain one of the most hallowed and cherished traditions of American life: the public's right to determine educational policy.

The reality is that neither the public nor the teachers are determining educational policy. The bulk of the enterprise is now run by budgetary exception. The costs of fuel, transportation, labor, and malpractice insurance and the mandates of the federal and state government preclude the exercise of independent judgment on all but a small portion of available resources. In states such as California where textbooks must be selected from state-adopted lists, the options are even narrower. Thus, the contention that the collective bargaining process will deprive the public of an ancient right is to some degree a phony issue.

This issue involves one of the surviving legacies of the 1960s: the concept that the representatives of the people are, in fact, not representative of the people, and therefore alternative or supplementary systems must be devised to authenticate the public interest. In its extreme forms, the loss of a board of education's perceived ability to represent the public interest led to a paralysis of agency government. Ironically, this breakdown did not lead to decision making in the street but helped trigger the rise of other and more distant agencies of government—the departments of education of the various states. The rise in relative power of these heretofore obscure bureaucracies has been one of the major developments in public administration during the 1970s—and one of the least remarked.

State departments of education have traditionally been the elephant burial grounds for aged superintendents. Since these agencies never did anything of consequence, good or bad, they were spared notice and criticism. During the 1960s, two related trends converged on these sleepy outposts. One was the need of the federal government for conduits at the state level to administer the flow of federal funds to local school districts. The second was the appearance of a new phenomenon at the local government level, an entity that can be called "publics." A public could be one person or fifty thousand persons. To qualify, it had to meet two criteria: it must be able to generate a media event, and it must not recognize the board of education as the agency to represent its views. Those publics on the fringe of sanity looked to what *Star Wars* calls the Force to guide their cause. The more effective publics, like lawyers, looked to the money as the means of wresting power from local boards. For example, in situations where there was no desegregation problem to bring in the federal judiciary, the remoteness of the U.S. Office of Education caused the state departments of education to fall heir to the task of limiting the power of the bad guys in office at the local level.

Enter collective bargaining.

Teachers are as much a public as Scientologists, the League of Women Voters, Jews for Jesus, or insurance brokers. We, too, were infected by the alienation of the 1960s. Added to this was an accumulation of professional and economic frustrations dating from World War II. Collective bargaining appeared to provide a rational and effective vehicle to meet our needs. The formula seemed sound. The board of education represented the people and hired a superintendent to manage the system. The teachers, by virtue of their professional training, did the best job possible, given the constraints imposed by the system. What could be more reasonable than that those working within the system should look to those operating the system for redress of grievances. The legislatures of thirty-one states agreed with this logic and enacted negotiation laws for teachers. Collective bargaining contracts have been reached at the local level in twelve additional states that do not have laws (see table 1).

The assumption among teachers, however naïve it may have been, was that, if the board of education lost its credibility with the people, the people would vote the rascals out. This assumption ignored the fact that accommodating the public as a whole is not at all the same as balancing the conflicting demands of organized publics.

The essential fallacy, of course, is the assumption that any faction with a megaphone constitutes a public; and, since all publics are inherently equal, all publics should have equal standing. How this insanity became conventional wisdom is speculation for a social psychologist. What we have witnessed is a progression from a belief in the

Table 1. Sunshine Laws and the Current Status of Teacher Bargaining Sessions under Legislation and Legal Rulings, by State

	Statutory Bargaining States	*Nonstatutory Bargaining States*	*Nonbargaining States*
Open Sessions Required	California Florida Minnesota		
Mutual Consent Required to Open Sessions	Iowa Maine Massachusetts Michigan Nevada Pennsylvania		
Closed Sessions Permitted	Alaska Connecticut Hawaii Idaho Montana Nebraska New Hampshire New Jersey New York North Dakota Oklahoma Oregon Texas Washington Wisconsin	Colorado Illinois Louisiana New Mexico Tennessee Wyoming	North Carolina
Status Unknown	Delaware Indiana Kansas Maryland Rhode Island South Dakota Vermont	Arkansas Arizona Kentucky Missouri Ohio Utah	Alabama Georgia Mississippi South Carolina Virginia West Virginia

Source: National Education Association, "Effects of 'Sunshine' Laws on Negotiations: An Analysis of Open Meeting Laws," *Collective Bargaining Quarterly* 2, no. 2 (January 1978): 29–35.

right to know; to a belief in the right to consult; to a belief in the right to determine. Although rarely stated in such bold terms, this progression may be as real as it is inevitable. It may be that when we say we want to know, in fact, we want to control.

What the more sophisticated publics believe is that the teachers, through the collective bargaining process, constitute a competitive public with an unfair advantage. But since the heyday of the 1960s, the number of competing publics in education has become reduced to a few hard-core special interest groups. Thus, the belief that teachers have a special advantage through collective bargaining is not a broad public sentiment but the attitude of limited insider publics whose own power is very real. Among these publics are the various manifestations of the Right to Work Committee and the organized parents of children in special education programs. In California, the battle for greater public participation in collective bargaining emanated from the League of Women Voters, the American Association of University Women, and Assemblyman John Vasconcellos. While this limited roster does not denigrate the intrinsic merit of public participation, it does underscore the fact that this is not an issue of great public passion. It is a squabble among élites.

Thus, when California adopted a collective bargaining law for teachers in 1975, the Rodda Act, it became only one of three states that mandate public bargaining (Florida and Minnesota being the others). This act, however, does provide for the consideration of publicly made proposals in private session. Section 3547 of the California government code details the duty to bargain openly:

(a) All initial proposals of exclusive representation and of public school employers, which relate to matters within the scope of representation, shall be presented at a public meeting of the public school employer and thereafter shall be public records.

(b) Meeting and negotiating shall not take place on any proposal until a reasonable time has elapsed after the submission of the proposal to enable the public to become informed and the public has the opportunity to express itself regarding the proposal at a meeting of the public school employer.

(c) After the public has had the opportunity to express itself, the public school employer shall, at a meeting which is open to the public, adopt its initial proposal.

(d) New subjects of meeting and negotiating arising after the presentation of initial proposals shall be made public within 24 hours. If a vote is taken on such subject by the public school employer, the vote thereon by each member voting shall also be made public within 24 hours.

(e) The board may adopt regulations for the purpose of implementing this section, which are consistent with the intent of the section; namely that the public be informed of the issues that are being negotiated upon and have full opportunity to express their views on the issues to the public school employer, and to know of the positions of their elected representatives.

The provisions in the collective bargaining law for California teachers merely reinforced existing law—the so-called Brown Act of 1953 (named after Ralph M. Brown who was not related to either of the Governors Brown)—and practice. On the whole, the Brown Act was beneficial, and any inconvenience it may have caused elected officials by denying them the right to meet in private was offset by the benefits of greater public access to information. If the Brown Act produced any surprises, it was the ease with which business as usual accommodated the new rules. Behavior among elected board members became more discreet but did not necessarily improve. On balance, the school administration would appear to have emerged stronger under the Brown Act than either the board of education or the public. With the board members denied the right to meet in executive session except on severely limited issues, the administrators became the conduits of information, proposals, and gossip between open board meetings and among the individual board members. In practice, the Brown Act served as a ready excuse for boards of education to delay or avoid dealing with teacher representatives during the pre-negotiation law era of the Winton Act, which lasted from 1965 to 1975. But, at the very most, the object of the Brown Act was public disclosure.

During the battle to attain a collective bargaining bill for teachers in 1975, many of the same questions being raised by this symposium were heard in the state legislature. There were advocates who believed that education was too important to be left on the bargaining table. It was feared that teachers would take over education. The compromise solution, section 3543.2 of the California code, was to limit the scope of bargaining to economic matters:

The scope of representation shall be limited to matters relating to wages, hours of employment, and other terms and conditions of employment. "Terms and conditions of employment" mean health and welfare benefits as defined by Section 53200, leave and transfer policies, safety conditions of employment, class size, procedures to be used for the evaluation of employees, organizational security pursuant to Section 3546, and procedures for processing grievances pursuant to Sections 3548.5, 3548.6, 3548.7, and 3548.8. In addition, the exclusive representative of certified personnel has the right to consult on the definition of educational objectives, the determination of the content of courses and curriculum, and the selection of textbooks to the extent such matters are within the discretion of the public school employer under the law. All matters not specifically enumerated are reserved to the public school employer and may not be a subject of meeting and negotiating, provided that nothing herein may be construed to limit the right of the public school employer to consult with any employees or employee organization on any matter outside the scope of representation.

The advocates of greater public involvement, on the other hand, viewed the new collective bargaining law as an opportunity to assert the public's role in determining educational policy, and so section 3547, quoted earlier, came into being. The California Teachers Association

(CTA), as might be expected, opposed both amendments to the act. While the CTA eventually had to swallow them in order to get a law, it viewed the limitation on scope of bargaining as the more significant amendment. Interestingly, many of the same people supported both amendments. One might have thought that if the objective was to use teacher collective bargaining as a vehicle for greater public involvement, it would follow that the public interest would be better served by having as wide a bargaining scope as possible—certainly not by excluding matters of educational concern. The political reality, of course, was that many supporters of these amendments were simply opposed to collective bargaining for teachers and ready to support any amendment that would weaken the law.

Regardless of the motives, section 3547 of California's collective bargaining law obviously represents a quantum leap from the presumed right to know. The public not only has the right to know the bargaining proposals, it has the right to respond to the proposals. Because of its experience with the Brown Act, CTA was not overly concerned about public intervention in the bargaining process. Public interest had been minimal except where busing and taxes were concerned. What CTA feared was that the section would provide boards of education leverage to avoid bargaining in good faith, that the noble experiment would become a bureaucrat's bargaining tactic. This is the fate that awaits most reform legislation, but that should not and, given the nature of reformers, will not discourage new efforts.

In the year since California's Public Employment Relations Board (PERB) adopted its regulations to implement section 3547, twelve complaints have come to the notice of the board, according to an unpublished survey compiled by the PERB staff. Considering that bargaining occurred in as many as three units per district for more than eight hundred school districts during the year, twelve complaints is certainly modest.

It is unfortunate that the interests that are opposed to public education on philosophical grounds, that are indifferent because they have no children in school, or that just do not want to pay taxes have been able to pit the strongest advocates of quality education against one another.

Beneath the apparent self-interest of every teacher in his or her economic survival is a hard core of idealism. Teachers have pride, and they want to succeed as teachers. One of the first lessons for an advocate of teachers' interests is that the members will not be satisfied with only economic gains. They want to be treated as professionals and given a chance to prove themselves. To broaden the scope of bargaining to allow teachers to negotiate matters of curriculum would not deny the public interest. It would let the public see, for the first time, the quality of the teachers it hires. No such judgment can now be made because, in our anxiousness to limit the power of the classroom teacher, we have denied him or her access to the decision making. It seems that a number of well-meaning publics, including teachers, have been milling about trying to influence boards of education with minimal effort. Through collective bargaining, the teachers appear to have a chance to make a break-through and move out of the pack. The other publics, for all that they are unhappy and frustrated with their own ability to influence events, have become more concerned with the possibility of teachers gaining influence than with seizing the opportunity to escalate the quality of the public debate on the future of American education that collective bargaining might provide.

Response

Comment by Kurt Hanslowe

It is a bit difficult to find a single theme in Ralph Flynn's charming paper. This is both a weakness and a strength. The weakness is the absence, when all is said and done, of an argument or a thesis other than that a wide scope of teacher bargaining is a good thing, although it is never made quite clear why this is so. The strength of such a paper is, of course, that it is not easy to analyze since its author so adroitly jumps from point to unconnected point. A well-written series of non sequiturs is one of the neater ways to keep from being found out.

One rather interesting thing does emerge: Flynn is not a democrat with a small *d*, he is an élitist. So is Harold Newman, for that matter, and so was Alexander Hamilton, whose spirit Newman invoked. Flynn views the political process as a squabble among élites. He concedes that collective bargaining gives one of those competing élites, the organized teachers, an unfair advantage. And, surprise of surprises, this is just as it should be, for teacher knows best, and what the rest of us should be doing, if we realized what was good for us, is to join the teachers in their attempt to move out of the pack, as Mr. Flynn puts it. The teachers' cause is, for some reason, really our cause, and we should be joining rather than opposing them.

No one outside Flynn's own élite comes off terribly well. Local officialdom is paralyzed; state education departments are elephant burial grounds for aged superintendents; the political opposition to collective bargaining is simply selfish or indifferent. Indeed, the general public doesn't exist at all. In other words, everyone, except his own élite, is either stupid or selfish or not even there; and if they are there, they are certainly not worth listening to. I guess if you are an élitist, that is how you are apt to view the world.

The problem I have with Flynn's view is his difficulty in perceiving political life as it really is in a democracy. Indeed, that problem has an "oughtness" dimension to it as well: How *ought* we to be running our affairs? On the one side, we find Flynn's world of inept bureaucrats and competing élites, with the teachers idealistically in the vanguard of improving both education and the quality of public debate in America. On the other side, we find a world of disgruntled citizen taxpayers and parents trying to restore the world of representative and town-meeting democracy.

Both these world views strike me as troublesome. The trouble with the second view is its otherworldliness. Returning to the good old days and ways seems difficult at best, and who knows how good those old days really were anyway. But I am not terribly happy with Flynn's view of the world either. Having my life run by a group of sophisticated, competing publics is not my idea of the good life. Also, it is not clear to me why the rest of us should enthusiastically endorse the bargaining process in public education.

Is it clear that teacher union goals are aimed at improving the quality of education? I am inclined to agree with Al Shanker that those goals at best are likely to be neutral with respect to educational quality. Is it clear that the stridencies and traumas of collective bargaining are likely to escalate the quality of public debate in America? Or perhaps I misunderstand what Flynn means by *escalation*. I am reminded of the story about Rudolph Bing, former director of the Metropolitan Opera, engaged in labor negotiations. After hearing the impassioned presentation of one union leader, Bing leaned back and said something like, "I didn't quite get that Mr. Jones; would you mind screaming it again!" Perhaps such stridency can be avoided if we take Flynn's advice and simply join hands with him. While this is an understandable aim from his point of view, I just do not see why all those various publics, other than the one he represents—some of which we have yet to hear from at this conference—can be expected to roll over and play dead. Thus, there is implicit in Flynn's world view increasing resort to power politics, with taxpayer revolts and demands by parents' organizations for laws and contracts to further their and their children's interests. I respectfully suggest that there is no difference in principle between a taxpayers' revolt to lower taxes and a teachers' strike to raise salaries. Both are power plays in pursuit of understandable economic self-interest.

Our difficulties derive in part, I think, from our failure to have devised a theory for the proper ingestion of collective bargaining by the processes of political democracy. We have some understanding of how these and related processes, such as party politics, are supposed to work. The political scientists have concerned themselves with these questions for a considerable time. We have also learned a good deal about collective bargaining in the private sector, about both the economic role it plays in the labor market and the sociological role it plays in industrial and commercial establishments. But we have thus far failed to come up with a satisfactory analytical tool or model to help us understand how an essentially economic process like collective bargaining fits into the essentially political processes of public finance and public administration. It is here that the industrial relations specialists have, in my opinion, been inexcusably remiss. Their endorsement of public sector bargaining was largely unthinking. Private sector institutions were uncritically transplanted into the public sector. This was done in the place of raising serious questions: Why should public employees get two cracks at the process of formulating public policy, one in the ballot box and another at the bargaining table? Is it because the public employee is both a citizen and an employee? What precisely are the roles of the various actors in the educational process? Who are the consumers? the children? the parents? How should the interest of nonparent taxpayers interact with that of nontaxpaying parents? Where should power repose among school boards, administrators, and education departments? What exactly is the nature of the pressures generated by a teachers' strike? Who precisely are the objects of those pressures?

When we begin to ask the right questions, perhaps we will be underway toward understanding the phenomenon of public sector bargaining and how it can be accommodated to the processes of political democracy.

Discussion Highlights

Elaborating his point that it is difficult to determine which citizens represent the public, Flynn described special interest groups as the principal vehicles of public influence and argued the infeasibility of the bargaining process accommodating all special interest groups. In response to Flynn's call to broaden the scope of bargaining, participants expressed concern that conditions of teacher employment would soon dictate public school curricula. Hanslowe's critique prompted participants to compare the private sector employer, who needs to balance the interests of labor and stockholders, with the public employer, who must respond to employees and citizens—*Editor.*

Ellen Ainsworth (Information Project on Educational Negotiations): Mr. Flynn, as the only other Californian in the room, I am quite concerned with your paper and with some of your comments. I notice that you start by calling California one of three states with open negotiations. I think you know as well as I do that what the law says is that negotiations *may* be open *only* if both parties agree. Having initial proposals introduced in public is not negotiating in public, as you or I or anyone else would define it.

You have asked what is the point of the various publics. I will try to tell you: When the state legislature meets and I want them to vote yes—or no—I can communicate with them. In the bargaining process, once it has gone secret, I cannot do so. I do not know how people have voted, nor do I know how the contract came about. You said that the prime thing in your mind is to cut a deal and get a decision made. The prime thing in my mind—whatever public I represent—is not the cutting of the deal. It is the cutting of the best possible deal for students, parents, and teachers. So we are at philosophical odds on the goal.

I view all this as a question of representative government. I would prefer, if not before then during and after negotiations, to be able to communicate my impressions to a school board and have some influence on the bargain. As the law calls for it, I don't have that chance. Your view of what is happening and my view are obviously very different, and this is something for us to argue in another forum. There is a dramatic increase in public participation, and I think the public is a lot smarter than you give them credit for being. If you wish to define *public*, I suppose my definition, unlike yours, would have to be "those people who are interested enough to understand this difficult project and show up and comment."

Ralph Flynn (California Teachers Association): The fact that we're here makes us by definition élites. We don't represent the public. We represent very special kinds of publics, quite selected ones. That was my point in looking at the spectrum of publics. They do range from the crazies—no one who has dealt with large communities doesn't recognize it. In the Los Angeles school district, we've dealt with the Maoists and the Progressive Labor Party—they are all there— they are all people, and we deal with them. But the price of accommodating their needs is destroying the society. I'm ready to premise that there are bounds beyond which we are not going to go. I think we are talking about responding to publics that are willing to buy at least some kind of societal consensus, so that limits it. As soon as you begin imposing this kind of limitation, you are changing the whole nature of the dialogue. We are talking about the very effective parent groups that go in and get the special legislation, the people we meet in the halls of the legislature, who lobby very effectively, who know the ins and outs, who have been around. This is where the battle lines meet. It is not widespread. Whether or not it should be is another issue.

Robert Bates (American Federation of Teachers): Professor Hanslowe, you concluded that we must ask the right questions. Which are the right questions? And what are the right answers to them?

Kurt Hanslowe (Cornell University): I tried at the end of my paper to suggest some kinds of questions I would begin to ask. I would probe more precisely into the nature of power relationships that are so involved in the public sector process. I would try to analyze precisely what exact role is being played by each actor in that process. I'd try to understand the nature of the pressures that are operative in that process. I would try to identify dissatisfied customers of the sort that knock on Mr. Newman's door and say, "We want to get in on this factfinding proceeding," and are told, "Well, no, you haven't a role to play in this procedure." I would then try to speculate on a possible procedure by which those outsiders could be given access without, at the same time, producing the sort of chaos Harold Newman was concerned about. Those are the directions in which I would try to press my speculations and my research.

The process of transplanting the whole collective bargaining process into public administration was done very quickly and in a kind of thoughtless way. It was simply assumed that exactly the same concepts and mechanisms would be appropriate with very little modification. There were only two major debates, and they were not conducted at a terribly sophisticated level. There was the sovereignty argument, which the public sector unions won in relatively short order; and since then there has been debate over whether or not you can have collective bargaining without the strike. Again transplanting private sector wisdom directly, the answer was plainly no, you can't have meaningful collective bargaining without having the pressures of the strike.

All the apparatus was picked up and transplanted because it was handy and convenient. How to refine that process, how to adjust to the circumstances—you *are* operating in a somewhat different setting from the setting in which General Motors operates—are questions on an unfinished agenda.

John Ryan (Philadelphia Federation of Teachers): When GM enters into negotiations—I just want to compare—not every stockholder has the right to come in and start bargaining. A stockholder does have the right to challenge it at the stockholders meeting, and the GM people who are sent in do have to answer questions. When we have public participation in collective bargaining, I can see the public having a voice, but it should be to the school board, which should be representing all the public. How the board wants to do that is up to them. But if we are going to bring in any group from the public that wants to take part in factfinding—aside from the cost of it—how much time are you going to spend if each group comes in to testify?

Kurt Hanslowe: GM does not pretend to be a democratic institution, so that is one reason why it is questionable to say, "What's good for GM is good for the whole country."

David Seeley (Public Education Association): Question to Mr. Flynn. Please address yourself to the California school site council issue. I'm puzzled as to why your organization wouldn't have welcomed greater teacher participation at the school level, the opportunity for teachers to engage as professionals in the discussion of school policy at the school level. Why would you be so opposed to that?

Ralph Flynn: First, we are not opposed to it the way you just described it. As with most programs like this, it is not the concept that is really being challenged, it is the specifics. We went through a heavy debate, for example, over the composition of the council and the precise balance. It appeared to us that what we had was a fragmented teacher representation, a fragmented representation of the community, and a cohesive administrative representation—one good person working full time will beat one good person working part time any day of the week. And what we saw happening in site after site was a cooption process. The central administrators—not as part of a nefarious plot but simply because they have the time to work on it—were able to form their power bloc. They could come in, for example, with a predrafted plan that the union then had to respond to, as well as the people at the site: "Why not? Who's got a better one?" So the system tended to falter.

The other issue is this: In any community action program one of the most critical ingredients is time. These programs take a lot of work. I believe in accommodation and adaptability. That is how organizations survive. If the school site council is where the play will go in California, that's where we're going to go. We will simply restructure our machine. If, in fact, the collective bargaining contract is going to be made at the school site level rather than the school district level, so be it. That's where we will shift the bargaining to. It's more cumbersome, more awkward, but we'll go where the power is.

Harold Newman (New York State Public Employment Relations Board): I want to make reference to something Kurt Hanslowe said. First, I agree with him that there should not be two bites of the apple. During the tenure of my predecessor, Bob Helsby, the then-permanent governor of New York State, Nelson Rockefeller, at our request, vetoed a bill that would have approved the hours of fire fighters by state statute. We said "Public sector unions, you get yourself a public sector bargaining law, and then you turn around and try to get another bite of the apple through the legislature. No way. What you seek you seek at the bargaining table."

The other concern I have is that we are seeking more from public access than public access can produce, even assuming that we could produce public access that works. Concomitant with examining questions of public access, we should also ask ourselves if, at the same time, we shouldn't be concerned with the forms that the efforts to maintain harmonious and cooperative relationships—to use the very lovely words of our own statute—between public employers and their unions require. I think we may be looking for too much with regard to public access. It seems important for us to keep in mind today and throughout tomorrow that there are some things between heaven and earth that are not going to be solved by having the public involved.

Vito Longo (New York State Education Department): I'd like to comment very briefly on Ralph's statement suggesting that the scope of bargaining be broadened to allow teachers to negotiate matters of curriculum. You have to understand that the union represents a group of people who have self-interest in mind—their continued employment, their salaries, and so on. To permit curriculum to be openly negotiated would, in situations where you have weak boards and very strong negotiating teams, have the long-term effect of having the subject matter provided to the children limited by the seniority or the job needs of people in strong positions within your leadership. That, to me, is frightening.

Ralph Flynn: You should remember that the bottom line of collective bargaining is that nobody has to. What you are permitting yourself to do is bargain. You are not committing yourself to buy. That is the essence of the collective bargaining process.

Robert Doherty (Cornell University): In this broadening of the scope and giving teachers more influence on professional matters, would you be willing to distinguish between teachers and the union?

Ralph Flynn: No. Tell me, how do you distinguish?

Robert Doherty: I'm just suggesting that the people with the greatest expertise in curriculum matters may not be the most active union members, or they may be—there is nothing contradictory about it. Is there going to be a union posture that we are going to have x courses offered in x ways or are there teachers as individual professionals who also have an interest?

Ralph Flynn: You're making a basic assumption that I think is a fallacy—that the union is inherently undemocratic.

Robert Doherty: No, I haven't thought that at all.

Ralph Flynn: If the union represents the teachers, it represents all the teachers. It represents the diversity of their views. Their concerns will surface.

III.

The Basis for a New Parent-Teacher Relationship in Collective Bargaining

David S. Seeley

Across the land parents and teachers are dismayed that, as collective bargaining becomes more widespread, relationships between parents and teachers are deteriorating. Support and cooperation are being replaced by distrust and hostility. The fruitless debates in recent years as to whether home or school is more to blame for learning failures have obscured the more fundamental truth: that successful education is based on neither the home nor the school alone but on a sound relationship between them. The prime outcome of the current deterioration in relations, therefore, is not the unhappiness of adults, whether teachers or parents, but the destruction of productive learning relationships for children.

Both parents and teachers have an interest in ensuring and maintaining such a learning relationship. The parents' interest is obvious. Whatever might be said about modern parents' neglect of their children, parents in every social class and walk of life have a strong instinctive concern for the welfare of their children and an interest in healthy and productive learning relationships in the school.

Likewise, teachers, almost without exception, prefer a strong learning relationship. Contrary to their growing reputation for selfishness and indifference, the vast majority of teachers come to their work wanting to be successful. Happily in this case, professional ideals coincide with satisfaction and comfort in the classroom. Nothing is more painful and wearing than spending six hours a day in unpleasant interaction with children. Unlike some workers for whom improved working conditions might mean less productive work habits, for teachers, the less productive the learning atmosphere of a school, the more intolerable are likely to be the working conditions—and vice versa, the more productive the classroom, the happier teachers will be.

There are many ways parents and teachers can work together to create a new partnership for learning. Since this is a conference on collective bargaining, I will discuss ways in which teacher contract negotiations can be changed to provide the basis for such a partnership. One is to develop a workable system for parent participation in the bargaining process, and the other is for parents and teachers to work, through the bargaining process, to reduce the bureaucratic disabilities that increasingly stifle productive learning relationships among parents, teachers, and students.

Underlying both approaches is the realization that an increasing number of important educational policy decisions are being made in collective bargaining, that these decisions are being made largely in secret, with little or no consultation with parents, and that many of the decisions, although proposed for the benefit of teachers, have the unintended effect of adding to the accumulation of centralized bureaucratic rules that obstruct both creative teaching and positive parent-student-teacher relationships.

Parent Participation in Collective Bargaining

The idea of parent participation in collective bargaining comes naturally from the idea of partnership itself. There should be no difficulty in seeing that the exclusion of parents from decisions vitally affecting their interests and those of their children greatly adds to their frustration and alienation. These feelings may take the form of disaffection with public education in general or with teachers, particularly when teacher bargaining is the cause for the exclusion.

In New York City, for instance, parents were furious when they learned that a new midwinter vacation had been agreed to in secret negotiations with the teachers' union with absolutely no parent consultation. They have also become increasingly disturbed by the degree to which effective operation of the schools, good supervision, in-service training, authority of the principal, and sound teacher assignments are obstructed by policies and procedures decided upon in such secret negotiations.

Parents are more recently beginning to realize that even the most traditional bread-and-butter issues of collective bargaining affect their interests as well as teachers'. An example of how this kind of parent consciousness is raised might look like this: Parents at P.S. XYZ become concerned when art instruction is severely cut because of budget reductions. They are informed that "while New York State spends an average of five dollars per year per student for art supplies, New York City spends an embarrassing 50 cents."[1] The parents are outraged. They turn to their state legislators indignantly to find out why the children of the city are so neglected and cheated. The legislators explain they have to deal with upstate legislators who confront them with the fact that the New York City school system spends considerably more than the state average per pupil expenditure, and if it can't buy adequate art supplies, it must be spending its money on other things. The parents begin to want to find out what these other things are and who determines budget priorities. They then learn that the city spends much more on debt service than other districts, in part because expenditures have exceeded revenues by hundreds of millions of dollars for a number of years. It also spends much more on pensions and maintains a more costly salary scale than even many wealthy suburbs. They also discover many of these budget priority decisions were not made as part of the budget process, which at least provides opportunities for public hearings, but were made instead in secret collective bargaining sessions, the results of which are often not disclosed even when the settlement is announced. The effect of these decisions comes out indirectly many months later when parents learn that "mandated costs," i.e., costs mandated by the contract, use up even the substantially increased revenues for which parents lobbied in the hope of improving educational services for their children.

It is easy to see, therefore, why there is legitimate demand for parent participation in bargaining decisions. It is not so easy, however, to satisfy it. The traditions of industrial labor relations are hostile to the involvement of third parties and to lifting the veil of secrecy surrounding the bargaining table. It is only in the last two or three years that steps have been taken to resolve these objections.

The first and most important step has been to recognize that public sector bargaining is basically different from industrial bargaining. While in the corporate world bargaining is an economic tug of war, with lost profits and lost wages as the pressure mounts, in the public sector it is a political process in which unions can apply political pressure on employers and in which work stoppages result not in lost profits but irate consumers of public services bringing political pressure to bear on elected officials to settle the dispute so services can be resumed.

As the joint Public Education Association/United Parents Association (PEA/UPA) project in New York City has discovered, public sector collective bargaining is really a fourth branch of government, separate

---

1. *Village Voice*, 6 June 1977, p. 61.

from legislative, judicial, and executive branches, yet making crucial public policy decisions. The fact that these decisions are made in secret and often hidden from the public for months after they are made, becomes intolerable in a democratic society.

Public sector collective bargaining is just as subject to the need for "open government" as other governmental functions; the specific remedies can go in several directions. One is to open the bargaining process, as in the case of the Florida "sunshine" procedure. Another is to televise bargaining sessions. A third is to bring representative public service consumers into the bargaining process itself. Both New York City and Rochester have had experience with this last technique, and both experiences are worth examining.

New York City, as a result of the Decentralization Law, has had, since 1970, three representatives of community school boards serving with two members of the central board of education on a five-person negotiating team. The three community representatives on the team report back to a full negotiating council representing all thirty-two community school boards. Although at first both the teacher union and the board representative feared such participation would interfere with the bargaining process, this has not occurred. The head of the teachers' union has, in fact, been quoted as saying that such representation has improved collective bargaining by helping community representatives become more informed about concerns of teachers and issues involved in negotiations. The context for involvement has clearly been improved, and this year's reversal of the midwinter vacation decision was a significant victory for parents.

While community school board involvement has not disrupted bargaining, it has not served particularly well to open the issues to broader discussion and participation either. Community school board members have had great difficulty in getting relevant information—and getting it in time—to participate effectively in bargaining decisions. They also have been denied the right to independent counsel and staff to assist them in participating effectively. They have had to rely upon the central board of education's staff, which is not always cooperative (and is sometimes suspected of being in collusion with the unions). Perhaps most important, the community school board representatives themselves have been placed under the traditional rules of secrecy in the negotiations and have been forbidden to discuss the issues with their local constituencies. As a result, there has been very little open political process for airing concerns and developing creative solutions.

The situation has been somewhat different in Rochester. There, with the active cooperation of the board's chief negotiator, a parent representative, nominated by parent groups, has not only been involved but has had the opportunity to go back to her constituency to discuss various points at issue in negotiations.

In neither New York City nor Rochester do parent or community representatives have legal authority to make collective bargaining decisions: they serve only in an advisory capacity with final authority for decisions left with the board of education. In both cases, however, they had some degree of influence as part of the bargaining team. The team usually tries to reach a unified position, and well-reasoned positions of the parent or community representatives are given considerable weight, particularly if backed up with a strong constituency. It is doubtful if the midwinter vacation would have been agreed to in New York City, for instance, if the matter had been discussed by the full negotiating council before it was decided, and it is almost certain it would not have been agreed to if the council had had the opportunity to bring the question back to parent and community groups for discussion. A great deal of bitterness toward teachers and the teachers' union could have been avoided if this route had been followed.

It can be argued that teachers have more chance of winning what they want if parents are not consulted. New York teachers did, after all, win a midwinter vacation for one year, by foreclosing discussions with parents. The whole point, though, is that such victories are not only illegitimate in terms of democratic government, they are also hollow for teachers, because they are won at the expense of increasing alienation of parents and citizens.

Our experience with parent and community participation, while spotty and far from satisfactory, indicates parent and community representatives can be involved in ways that both respect the rights of the various parties and help to strengthen the partnership between parents and teachers. There is no consensus yet, however, as to the best way to achieve this. In particular, there is still considerable debate whether it is better for parent and community representatives to participate in negotiations as third parties, with their own independent vote on the contract, or as part of the management side of the bargaining table.

The third-party approach sounds at first more attractive for several reasons. It seems to give the parent or community representatives more power, since they could presumably make decisions independent of the board of education. It also seems to be less antagonistic to teachers, since parents would be free to agree with either the labor or the management side of the table, rather than being identified with the necessarily adversarial management posture.

There are serious questions, however, as to whether a third-party system would work. Collective bargaining is inherently a two-party relationship between a group of employees and their employer, and it may be that only these two parties have the actual power to conclude an agreement. So long as employees are willing to work under terms offered by the employer, and so long as the employer is willing to offer such terms, a deal can be struck between these two prime parties regardless of what any third party might think.

Third parties who are not participating in the negotiations are, of course, free to try to influence either party. They certainly are free to agree, and often have, with teachers as well as with a board of education. But when push comes to shove, when parents want to go beyond just pleading with the parties and actually participate in the bargaining decisions, they may have no choice but to recognize that the union necessarily represents the employees' interests, and the only way to bring parent interests to the bargaining table with any real power is as part of the management side of the table, as part of the entity that has the power to grant or withhold terms of employment. From this point of view, the proper course for parents is to try to institutionalize a more influential power relationship with the board of education through effective representation on the management side of the table.

In New York City, the joint PEA/UPA Collective Bargaining Task Force has taken this latter course. There is no realistic prospect of parents gaining an independent veto on contract agreements, and the task force is trying to develop procedures whereby parents and citizens can have more opportunity to influence management's bargaining position. This in no way precludes parent groups from trying to develop more understanding and more cooperative relationships with teachers; it is only a recognition that parents sometimes have different interests than teachers, interests they cannot realistically expect the teachers' union to represent. The board of education, however, does purport to represent parent interests as well as the interests of the rest of the public, and parents can legitimately press the board not only to represent them on specific issues but also to establish better procedures on a continuing basis.

The most important procedures in this regard are those that would open the consideration of contract issues to informed discussion, both before the negotiations begin and during the contract talks themselves, as possible areas for compromise become clearer. The desirability for greater openness derives from the basic democratic right for citizens to participate in public policy decisions; from the opportunity open discussion would provide for more creative solutions; and from the need for parents to develop an informed constituency.

It may be that public hearings at one or more points in the bargaining process would be desirable for open discussion of the issues. The California experience, with required disclosure of both union and board demands and public consultation before the beginning of bargaining, will be instructive, but as with so many cases of legally mandated consultation, the spirit in which boards of education undertake these procedures will be of prime importance in determining their effectiveness. Boards of education have often been slow to recognize the advantage of an informed constituency on collective bargaining issues. They are sometimes more jealous in defending the secrecy and exclusiveness of bargaining than are teachers. Nevertheless, mandated procedures for disclosure and consultation are probably desirable parts of the package of needed reforms. Beyond the mandates, however, boards of education probably need both pressure and help from parent and citizen groups to develop ways of presenting information and conducting discussions to provide the greatest opportunity for airing and resolving differences.

Since procedures for parent participation are not yet established, there is an opportunity for teacher and parent organizations to cooperate and develop a workable system to bring concerns of both groups to the table, so they can be understood by all parties, so solutions can be found in cases where interests conflict, and so final settlements will be more likely to be accepted as fair by all parties. It may seem naïve to expect teacher organizations to cooperate in finding ways for parents to have more voice, but parents will increasingly demand and gain more voice in any case, and as I have pointed out, it is in the interest of teachers for them to get it and to get it in ways that will be the most constructive. Teachers may well find parents their allies on many issues and vice versa.

Parent-Teacher Assault on Bureaucracy
There are other substantive issues in which parents and teachers can find common interest. One that deserves particular attention is the need to reduce the negative effects of bureaucracy in education.

The bureaucratic organizational model, which provides the fundamental structure of contemporary public school systems, has been carried too far. In fact, it may be the wrong model altogether for education, which depends so much on human relationships and the interaction of forces inside and outside the educational system. The real education system is the society at large: the schools can play their part only if they are integrally related to the other social forces that educate children. The effort to build a separate, self-contained, and rationalized bureaucracy to educate children tends to separate the schools from the society necessary to make them work and to dehumanize their operations for students and teachers alike.

Bureaucracy undoubtedly has its uses, and for some functions, multilayered management, rigid rules and regulations, and a pyramidal hierarchy of authority may provide the best organizational structure. But by and large, it does not work for the primary functions of a school system: teaching, learning, and the creation of a supportive relationship between teachers, students, home, and school. The bureaucratic mentality and procedures often obstruct these functions. How many times have we seen creative teachers or principals either frustrated in their work or driven from the schools altogether because they did not fit into the bureaucratic mold? And the extreme cases in which a teacher or principal rebels openly are only the tip of the iceberg. What happens day in and day out in our public schools is a pervasive and persistent obstruction and deadening of effective educational processes.

The issue of bureaucratization comes up in collective bargaining because, without intending it, the collective bargaining process itself tends to increase the bureaucratization of school systems. Problems affecting teachers in various ways throughout a school are crystallized into systemwide demands and then translated into new systemwide rules and regulations. Because some principals play favorites in the assignment of teachers, rules are devised for assignment by seniority or rotation. Because some in-service training programs are too burdensome or meaningless, restrictions are placed on nonclassroom activities. Because some supervision and teacher evaluation are heavy-handed, rules are laid down on what can and cannot be done in this area. The abuses are real enough, but their solution through a systemwide collective bargaining agreement exacts a heavy price in terms of loss of flexibility at the school level and in terms of the atmosphere and mentality of the system as it becomes ever more standardized and bureaucratized.

There is irony in this development. The unionization of teachers was in part a reaction against the increasing bureaucratization of school systems. Teachers were treated as the least important cogs in the machine, the lowest rung on the bureaucratic ladder. They found increasing difficulty in making their voices heard as power shifted to the top. Yet the instrument chosen to respond to this, the collective power of teachers applied to the top decision-making centers of the system, has not returned more power to the individual teacher. Instead, it has enabled teachers, acting collectively through their union organization, to participate in the centralized rule-making behavior of the system.

How can parents and teachers work together to reverse this tendency? The first step is to recognize the problem, to see how bureaucratization is undermining the educational process and human relations among parents, teachers, and students.

The second step is for parents to recognize that there are real abuses that teachers can suffer from poor administration and supervision and that it is in their interest to find ways to protect teachers from these abuses, but ways that will not increase the bureaucratic rigidities and administrative arteriosclerosis of the system. One way is for both interest groups to work together to make sure principals are highly qualified, not only in terms of expert knowledge but in terms of leadership ability and fairness and integrity with teachers and students. Another way might be to have some kind of informal hearing process, which might include parents on the hearing panel, to hear charges of administrative abuse, rather than trying to prevent all abuses by inflexible and oppressive rules.

A third step is for parents and teachers to work together to develop a better decision-making process at the school level, one in which both parent and teacher concerns can be better heard and worked out within a context where parties with a mutual interest in long-term harmonious relations have an opportunity to get to know each other personally. There are those who say neither the central bureaucracy nor union leaders will agree to increased decision making at the school level because both would lose power from such a development. It remains to be seen how true this might be. There is at least some chance that both school and union leaders are beginning to see that past trends toward increased centralization and bureaucratic control are leading to a dead end and must be changed if the educational process is to be revitalized, teachers elevated to true professional status, and a strong partnership established between teachers and parents. Both school administrators and union leaders should have no difficulty in retaining important leadership roles for themselves—even if somewhat different roles than at present—if they take the initiative in helping to reshape public education along less bureaucratic lines.

The nature of collective bargaining would undoubtedly change with such a debureaucratizing effort by teachers and parents. Fewer educational decisions would be made in the pressure-cooker, adversarial climate of the bargaining table. More would be made on a cooperative basis between teachers, parents, students, and administrators at the school level. The strength of the union as a systemwide organization would remain important; this power, however, would be used not to push through specific centralized rules and procedures but to make sure teachers are properly involved at the school level, not overshadowed, bullied, or exploited by administrators, or by parents, for that matter. If teachers and parents are working closely, at both the school and system levels, they might well reinforce each other's claims for better involvement in decision making at the school level. Both groups have complained about bureaucratic attitudes and petty rules that obstruct good teaching and human relationships with individual children, but they have too seldom exploited this common interest as a basis for unity.

The teacher power movement, like all such movements, has its limits, and these limits are rapidly being reached as parents and citizens become disaffected. Teachers can go only so far without public support, and parents, despite their differences on some issues, are their most natural allies. A new partnership between parents and teachers will come to be seen as not only educationally desirable but politically practical. Adjusting the collective bargaining process to increase parent participation and diminish the bureaucratizing effects of collective bargaining will facilitate such a partnership.

Sunshine Bargaining: The Case for Public Participation

Donald Magruder

In public education, the collective bargaining movement gathered up steam and began moving in earnest in the early 1960s, with Albert Shanker's New York City strike for the right to bargain. Since that time, a majority of state legislatures have conceded to this movement in one way or another. In 1978, Tennessee adopted a collective bargaining law in education, thus allowing collective bargaining to invade the last bastion of America holding out against this form of personnel relations, the South. (Although Florida has had a comprehensive collective bargaining law since 1974, this southernmost of southern states can hardly be considered part of the South.)

It was inevitable that a force as volatile, powerful, and personal as collective bargaining in education would give birth to a counterforce. As the Florentine statesman Francesco Guicciardini put it, "Those who meddle in plots should bear in mind that nothing is more fatal to their success than the endeavor to make them too safe." As teacher union leaders tie up administrators and school boards, increase militancy, strike against the public, elect public officials, and otherwise become successful in accomplishing their ambitious goals, they are also creating a counterforce, the American parent and citizen.

The Motivation behind the Counterforce

Probably the biggest mistake being made by educators today is their failure to listen. The problem is that, for years, educators have been talking to themselves and not to the general public. This could be compared to my perception of the 1976 presidential campaign. Everyone I talked with discounted Jimmy Carter as a viable candidate for president. Obviously, I was talking to the wrong people. It is much the same with educators. Educators listen to each other but do not listen to the citizen.

If educators would listen to the citizens and parents, here is what they would be hearing:

1. Public education is too expensive. Citizens and parents are feeling the pinch of inflation. Because inflation also affects the schools and costs increase, the pressure grows. Parents and citizens will point out that during the past twenty years teacher salaries have tripled and quadrupled, making the highest percentage gains of any occupational group in our country. It matters not that the teacher salary began at a much lower base than other workers; this fact is quickly forgotten by those who must lower their standards of living because of inflation. Inflation, of course, causes higher taxes for the support of public schools as well as for other public services. It is not necessary to examine here the failure rate for bond and millage referenda at the local level. The passage of a bond or millage proposition is almost a thing of the past. The rejection rate of these elections points out only too well the attitude of the public. The most immediate place for rejection is a local election, where the citizens can at least be heard loud and clear.

2. The public schools have failed to produce. Public schools were established to teach the young, to pass on to the next generation the learning necessary for that generation to continue past progress and to develop a new and better society. At present, citizens do not believe that public education is producing results. They have much evidence to support their contention. In August 1978, the *St. Petersburg Independent* reported that one-third of the teachers applying for positions in a metropolitan school district failed to pass an eighth-grade exam. It was reported that these potential teachers will be given two more opportunities to pass the test.[1]

Other motivating forces behind citizen and parent interest in becoming involved in collective bargaining in education are the schools' lack of sensitivity to the needs of the public; a general lack of trust of public officials; and a reaction to voter indifference and apathy.

How Do Parents and Teachers Differ?

The ideas of teachers and teacher organizations about education differ greatly from those of citizens and parents. The education "profession" has developed its own ideas about what is best for children. These ideas are passed along from professor to teacher, teacher to teacher, and administrator to teacher. Rarely are they passed from parent to teacher because the schools have become a defensive public service that closes ranks, moves the wagons into a circle, and prepares for the assault.

---

1. "Teachers Fail Test," *St. Petersburg Independent*, 12 August 1978.

Here are some of the key issues on which parents and teachers differ:

1. Social promotion. Our modern society has encouraged the easy way out. Teachers say, "If a child cannot pass your class send him on to the next. Maybe he is a late bloomer and will catch up next year."

2. Grouping by ability. Teachers say, "Give me my fair share of the slow learners and no more," and "Besides, it's anti-American to group by ability anyway." It matters not that the slower group stays slow and the gifted are bored with it all.

3. Curriculum. Teachers say, "Teachers are trained professionals, and they know best what should be taught and how it should be taught." Never mind who owns the schools.

4. Testing for students. Teachers say, "Minimum functional literacy tests are unfair and unreliable."[2] Teachers and teacher organizations oppose testing of students for comparative purposes, even minimum competency examinations.

5. Testing for teachers. Teachers ask, "Are physicians tested periodically? Are lawyers tested after they have passed the bar examination? Of course not, and since teaching is a profession, teachers shouldn't be tested either." How competent are our nation's teachers? Parents have no way of knowing if their child's teacher is competent. Teachers and teacher organizations oppose periodic testing to weed out incompetents. Parents can change physicians or lawyers at will, but just try to get your child transferred out of a class with a teacher that is believed incompetent.

I do not wish to paint the entire profession with the incompetency brush. The majority of teachers in our nation are competent, in my opinion. The purpose of a teacher organization or union, however, is to protect and defend its members. That is why the organization exists, and that is how it earns its dues from the teacher member. It is, in the opinion of a teacher union, management's job to weed out incompetent teachers, and the union will protect each member, competent or incompetent.

The procedure that the union employs to protect and defend incompetent teachers is the collective bargaining contract. The collective bargaining contract is where the taxes go. The contract establishes the workday, the fringe benefits, the personnel policies, the teacher evaluation, the school calendar, student discipline procedures, and even what time of day families in the district rise. These decisions are made at the collective bargaining table as agreements between the teacher union and the management representatives. These decisions, in most instances, are made in secret, behind closed doors. The parties to the contract tell the

---

2. "On Eve of Hearing, Professor Calls State Tests Unfair, Unreliable," *St. Petersburg Times*, 15 August 1978.

public that collective bargaining will not work unless the parties can meet in secret to give and take. The problem is that there has been too much giving on the part of management and too much taking on the part of the unions, and before the public knows anything at all about it, it is too late.

In a word, the primary motivating force behind demands for greater public access to the bargaining table is frustration.

A Representative Counterforce

How can leaders in education recognize that the citizens and parents developing into a counterforce are legitimate representatives of the public? We have been informed, with some validity, that a public school's constituency is composed of many subgroups. We could list dozens, depending on how definitive we would like to be. Which of these subgroups really speak for the people? An oversimplified answer to this question is that all of them do but none of them does completely.

An illustration might support this: Recently I worked in a school district selecting a new superintendent. The screening committee held four public hearings to determine community consensus in different sections of the school district. The public hearings were well attended, but it suddenly dawned upon the committee that they were seeing and hearing from the same people, no matter what section of the community they visited. It was obvious that one segment of the community was well organized, vocal, and hardworking. It was also apparent to the committee that if there were other opinions within the community they must be sought out by a method other than public hearings. This experience brought out the fact that there existed within the community a comparatively small segment of the population with highly defined goals. These goals, however, were not typical of the general population.

This vignette points out the need for careful analysis to assure that those representatives of the citizens and parents who claim to represent the public really do. Public officials are often swayed by a vocal minority: for example, the public official who states that "I had dozens of telephone calls about this issue," when in reality this person received one or two calls at most. It is most important that, in collective bargaining in education, the representatives of the public be truly representative. In my opinion, the best methods devised, to date, to ensure proper representation are the citizens' committee; full public information before, during, and after negotiations; and school-by-school reporting. Let us examine these methods one at a time.

First, a citizens' committee should be established to represent the public during negotiations. Policies should be adopted and procedures implemented to ensure this committee is a cross section of the community. The committee should be, as nearly as possible, a microcosm of the community, reflecting its mix of ethnic backgrounds, races, sexes, and levels of education. Organizations should be invited to submit names of representatives for the committee. Individuals representing subgroups such as senior citizens, elementary and secondary school parents, non-parents, and others should be included. The citizens' committee should be small enough to be effective and large enough to be representative.

The purpose of the committee is to monitor collective bargaining in education, from the receipt of the union's demands to the final signing of the contract, and to notify the participants, the public, and the public's elected representatives of the community's desires with respect to the collective bargaining contract.

This committee can watch over negotiations and provide the communication necessary to keep the community informed about what is being negotiated. If the school board is giving away too much of the authority vested in it by the electorate, the citizens' committee should inform the public. If the collective bargaining contract squeezes out public input about curriculum, the workday, discipline, class size, teacher evaluation, transfer, promotion or assignment, and other employment conditions affecting publicly financed education, the committee should not permit its ratification. If the representatives of the public do not demand and obtain, quid pro quo, practices that will improve the educational process in the community, the citizens' committee should inform the community. Finally, if public officials do not insist on "a fair day's work for a fair day's pay," the public should know about it. Our modern society has devised methods of determining productivity. It is now time to use these methods in public schools.

School-by-school reporting is most helpful in keeping the public informed. School advisory committees can report, on a regular basis, the condition of learning within an individual school center and can learn firsthand the effects of a collective bargaining contract upon the education of children. School administrators, generally, do not look with much enthusiasm upon school advisory committees because it is "easier" to operate without them. A properly constituted school advisory committee working within prescribed perimeters, however, can actually become a highly supportive source of communication with the public.

Public Involvement in Collective Bargaining
The answer to a nervous public counterforce is public bargaining. The mystique of collective bargaining is shattered by the light of day. Collective bargaining contracts in which the rights of parents are bought and sold cannot stand a fishbowl atmosphere. Sunshine bargaining in the public sector can and does work.

Since 1974, Florida has had a public collective bargaining law that requires the parties to meet and negotiate in open sessions. The school board and its chief negotiator may meet in executive session to establish ground rules and to be informed about the progress of negotiations, but actual negotiations must take place in public. Other states have been watching the experiment in Florida, and the state legislature of Tennessee, after studying Florida's experience, required collective bargaining to be performed in public.

States with longer histories of public sector collective bargaining are now taking a serious look at sunshine bargaining. Many of the states preparing second or third generation bargaining laws will be considering public collective bargaining as the public counterforce increases in intensity. Minnesota now requires open bargaining, except in instances exempted by the director of the public employee relations board. California has altered its law to require that union demands be made public a decent interval before negotiations commence. Many localities are also experimenting with open collective bargaining sessions. The trend is definitely toward bringing public negotiations out of the closet.

When public collective bargaining was a new phenomenon in Florida, both management and the union negotiators were inexperienced. The first year, Florida had many problems bargaining in the sunshine. Participants played to the audience. Teacher unions packed places of negotiation with supporters, often using hand signals for cheers or jeers. Tentative agreements often polarized positions and hardened postures. School district weaknesses were exposed to the public before management had a chance to correct them. The process was more time-consuming because the chief negotiators were required to couch their arguments in a way that would not be misunderstood by the press and the public. Adversary relations were emphasized because the players' positions had to be obvious to their supporters.[3]

Despite these disadvantages, however, a survey of the attitudes of the parties involved proved positive toward open negotiations. School board members, two to one, believed in open negotiations; the great majority of school superintendents also favored bargaining in the sunshine despite the year that they had just gone through. On the management side, only the chief negotiators were opposed to sunshine bargaining by a slight majority. Both teacher unions, the National Education Association and the American Federation of Teachers, are on record as opposing open negotiations.

The public took little interest in the teacher negotiations:

---

3. Donald R. Magruder, *Bargaining in Public: Help or Hindrance*, special report (Washington, D.C.: Labor-Management Relations Service, 1976), p. 8.

One can conclude from the reports of the negotiators that members of the public, or parents, or "taxpayers" had better things to do than to attend collective bargaining sessions. Perhaps they relied upon the media to attend and report on the progress of the process. Perhaps, since it was the first year of formal collective bargaining, the public was not motivated sufficiently, to attend the meetings. One thing was certain, however, the citizen was in no hurry to join the participants at the collective bargaining table.[4]

The study quoted above was conducted in 1975. Nineteen seventy-eight has brought about a significant change. First, sunshine bargaining is accepted as being successful. With a little experience under their belts, both management and union negotiators have become at ease with open bargaining. The showy aspects of earlier years are things of the past. With few exceptions, none being blamed on open bargaining, collective bargaining in education is proceeding smoothly and with minimum trauma. The negotiators on both sides have gained much experience and sophistication in the bargaining process. The collective bargaining mystique, born and fostered by negotiators, has also worn off.

There are other changes as well. Citizens are now becoming involved. The Florida Congress of Parents and Teachers has noticed that, in most of its localities, when its members appear before the school board to make a request, the school board's hands are tied, not by the state department of education as was the case before but now by a fully guaranteed, legal collective bargaining contract, enforceable in court. So, the PTA, which has become mainly a parents' organization since collective bargaining, has decided to become a counterforce. The leadership of PTA has sponsored statewide and local workshops on collective bargaining in education. Parents are determined to learn as much about the process as possible. Local chapters are organizing parents to attend all collective bargaining sessions. With the training parents are receiving, they will know what they are looking for. PTA members vow that they will monitor the sessions and report back to the public, and to the school board, their views about what is being bargained away.

It need not be the PTA in your state. The counterforce may be any citizen group that becomes sufficiently motivated to protect the interest of public education from the vested interest of teacher labor unions.

One thing about America, our democracy has a way of working. Sometimes it just takes a while.

---

4. Ibid., p. 9.

Response

Comment by Ronald Donovan

I approach the issue of citizen participation in collective bargaining as a skeptic, not so much because of doubts that there is reason for concern that legitimate interests of the public may not be adequately reflected in the process, but rather because of great uncertainty about how the goal can be achieved. Thus I share some of the concerns expressed by David Seeley and Donald Magruder but am doubtful that either of them offers us a reasonable and workable scheme for dealing with the question. In terms of the analysis of the problem, it seems to me that Seeley provides us with a valuable insight when he speaks of the bureaucratization of the schools.

The papers diverge on two significant matters. Magruder seems to find the teachers responsible for most, if not all, of the educational system's failings and, by doing so, exculpates management. Seeley, on the other hand, is much more generous-spirited, more evenhanded, in distributing blame. Moreover, he acknowledges that teacher and public interests are not inherently antithetical. The second major difference between the papers goes to the question of how best to make the citizen interest felt in the process of bargaining. Seeley would have community influence exercised through the management side of the table, while Magruder urges participation of the public as a third party, independent of either the union or management.

There are a number of shortcomings in Magruder's analysis and prescription. First among them is the problem of identifying what he terms a "representative counterforce," of distinguishing those who are "truly representative" of the community from those who may be false claimants. Merely bestowing the label *citizen's committee* upon a group offers no assurance that it is any more representative of community opinion than the "well organized, vocal, and hardworking" people who kept reappearing at public hearings in the episode he recounts.

Magruder expresses complete confidence in the ability of the citizens to gauge the effects of collective bargaining upon the educational program and to prescribe the needed remedies for any perceived shortcomings. According to him, what needs to be done is to ascertain through regular observation how the implementation of the teacher contract affects the children's education; to apply the concept of a fair day's work for a fair day's pay; and to see that the methods of productivity improvement are applied to the school enterprise. Presumably by accomplishing these tasks, most of the problems of the schools will dissolve. Desirable goals these may be, but the achievement of any one of them is not the simple task that he would have us believe. The determination of a fair day's pay, for example, poses no problem for him, even though it has confounded philosophers and economists for centuries.

Magruder indicts teachers and their organizations for many of the ailments of the schools, for the espousal of social promotion, for resistance to curricular changes and minimum competency examinations, and for the failure to weed out the incompetent among them. These charges seem to beg these questions: What are the school boards and administrators doing while all this is taking place? Doesn't management bear some responsibility for these problems? Isn't it primarily management's responsibility to rid the system of incompetent teachers? To be sure, collective bargaining can make changes in the system more difficult, but it seems patently unfair to lay all these shortcomings at the teachers' doorstep or to attribute them to collective bargaining. Indeed, I suspect that most of these problems antedate the development of bargaining.

On the basis of the evidence in Magruder's paper, what do we have to commend bargaining in the sunshine, to persuade the unconvinced that it leads to negotiated settlements which are responsive to the interests of the public? After four years, Magruder is unable to report much in the way of public involvement in negotiations, except to say that the Florida PTA is vowing that it will become involved. Although the idea has won the support of school board members and superintendents, it is not popular with the management and union negotiators. This puts one in mind of the gladiatorial contests during Roman circuses. The fans thought they were great, only the gladiators were unenthusiastic. Negotiators on both sides are reportedly more at ease with open bargaining, having gained experience and sophistication in the process. The question that occurs to me is whether this greater ease is attributable less to satisfaction with open bargaining than to the bargainers having come upon ways to negotiate privately.

In one of his concluding statements Magruder offers what strikes me as a final irony:

There are other changes as well. Citizens are now becoming involved. The Florida Congress of Parents and Teachers has noticed that, in most of its localities, when its members appear before the school board to make a request, the school board's hands are tied, not by the state department of education as was the case before but now by a fully guaranteed, legal collective bargaining contract, enforceable in court.

Thus, after four years of "sunshine," it would appear that little has changed.

Discussion Highlights

The papers by Seeley and Magruder turned participants first to the question of teacher professionalism and whether it had been furthered or hindered by collective bargaining. They then debated at greater length the public's need for more information about bargaining in the schools than is currently provided. Here, a few of the participants sought to make a distinction between *secrecy* and *privacy* in negotiations—*Editor.*

Francine Herman (Cornell University): In New York State we require what amounts to a landslide vote in any election, 60 percent, to do anything about the tax rate, so that school board position, which used to be considered an honorary position, is now an extremely political position. We are trying to impose on that old structure, the school board, the twentieth-century collective bargaining mode. Is it possible to continue that way? Everybody talks about professionalism, but can you apply the same rules to employed professionals as you can to self-employed professionals? I think not.

Donald Magruder (Florida School Boards Association): You brought up something that has concerned me for a long time now, the problem of professionalism. Under Florida collective bargaining law a teacher is a public employee. I think that when the change was made by the profession to go to the use of collective bargaining, that took something away from the professionalism of other years.

Francine Herman: What I am asking is, Can the structure of school boards and organized teachers continue to be the modus operandi? But, to get to your point, let me say that I think the good old days had so much paternalism that it was shocking. What you are saying is that now we no longer have the right to be paternalistic about our teachers. I think it is a jolly good thing that we don't.

David Seeley (Public Education Association): Teachers' unions grew in part because we had public education that did not respect the notion of teachers as professionals. It may have respected them as good-spirited ladies who would work for $2,000 a year without complaining, but I don't think that, by and large, the school districts treated teachers as real professionals. The last fifteen years have seen an increase in professional aspirations of teachers. They had been getting increasing amounts of education and wanted to be viewed as professionals, and the system was simply not responding to that. I would argue that collective bargaining is a response to a structure that is still the problem. It never did see teachers as professionals. But collective bargaining is not helping them get through as professionals, either. So making collective bargaining go away or finding ways you can get public access to bargaining won't deal with that problem.

John Dunlop (National Education Association): Dave, you talked about secrecy in bargaining. Maybe you can comment on what you perceive to be the cause of it in New York City. Is it the peculiar environment that bargaining operates in there that makes secrecy more rampant than in a lot of other places? Or is secrecy part and parcel of the collective bargaining process, irrespective of the environment that it happens to be working in? What is your view on it?

David Seeley: I have been assuming that secrecy was inherent in the bargaining process. When we try to get it changed, people who have expertise in this area, like Harold Newman, say that you can't bargain except in secret, that it won't work. Now maybe there is something peculiar about New York City, but as far as I can tell, secrecy is a very common problem. It is exacerbated in New York City by one very crucial factor, the collusive nature of the structure. For we do have a board of education that is not selected by the unions but is working behind the scenes in collusion with them— which is what I really think happened in New York City for ten years. There really is a very close political connection between the people on both sides of the table, and they really are working out a deal that will satisfy their view of their political operations. That certainly contributes to secrecy.

I do want to say that I'm not against the "sunshine" possibility. I'm trying to announce that I feel resolute that there has got to be information. How you get it, I'm not sure. But unless the negotiations experts of the unions and the boards of education can come up with a better way, I'm going to go for "sunshine," because that, at least, is one way you can find out what is going on.

John Dunlop: Part of the Taylor Act was made to let the public be apprised of the dimensions of the dispute and the rationale behind the proposals of the parties. It has fallen in disfavor for a lot of reasons. But if we are looking at public knowledge about what is going on in bargaining, I would argue that you have it here in New York.

David Seeley: How many issues go to factfinding? Most bargaining doesn't go to factfinding. The deal is cut without factfinding ever entering into it. And even if the issue does go to factfinding, then to what extent does that give you a window on what actually transpired in the bargaining?

John Dunlop: I would say that is part and parcel of the ability of the factfinder to write.

David Seeley: This may be a fruitful area where we can really make some progress this afternoon. It was Harold Newman's view—and I would say it is a very common view among labor mediators—that factfinding is really a part of the process of mediation, to try to help two parties get together. And we were just discussing during the break this morning that if there really is a problem with the political process as opposed to the collective bargaining process, maybe factfinding could be modified somewhat so that it would be used for informing the public. Four or five years ago when I tried to find out what a factfinder's report was, they said no, there was a ten-day waiting period.

Harold Newman (New York State Public Employment Relations Board): It's five in New York City.

Ellen Ainsworth (Information Project on Educational Negotiations): It's ten in California.

David Seeley: We said, "Hey, we want to find out what you came up with as the facts," and they said, "No, it's just for the two parties." That's my opinion of what factfinding is up to now. It's not facilitating public disclosure.

Ellen Ainsworth: We have talked this morning and again this afternoon about who is the public and what is representative. Is there any possibility that we can agree that the public is anyone who comes and who cares? There seems to be some sort of a hangup with the word *representative*. If I don't show and I'm not represented, that's my fault. I would like to lay to rest this whole question of representatives. The people who really care are going to show, and they are going to exert political pressure. If we can adjust this process to make room for those people, grand. If we can't, then I too am going home and start talking third party at the table.

David Seeley: I'm really saying the same thing Ellen is. That is, within the realm of access, without talking about a specific designated or elected representative, those who feel their interests are affected by the information they have need to get some way of being able to get the word to the negotiators about how they feel about it. If we can't agree upon who should represent the public, how they would participate at the table, let's see if we can get agreement with regard to the political process. The public is anybody out there who feels interested in the facts about the factfinding.

Happy Fernandez (Parents' Union for Public Schools in Philadelphia): The problem is that would tend to favor some children and families because for a low-income family, a single-parent family, or a two-parent family where both parents are working it's really difficult to participate.

Robert Bates (American Federation of Teachers): I'm rapidly getting in a quandry about what the purpose of collective bargaining is. The more that is said here, the more I'm convinced that almost everyone here believes it is to inform the public or to provide for all kinds of public participation in the determination of wages and benefits and certain other conditions of employment. I was always under the impression that collective bargaining was a process between the parties who represent the public and the parties who have to live under those conditions—an alternative to absolute paternalism. We know paternalism didn't work, at least as far as wages and benefits and conditions for employees are concerned. I thought the purpose of collective bargaining was to bring about agreement on such things, but we are talking about it as a process to determine that great big educational policy in the sky. Certainly collective bargaining affects certain kinds of educational policy. Educational policy also affects terms and conditions of employment. But the more this discussion goes on, the more I hear concern about perpetuating altercations between the various interest parties rather than bringing about the resolutions of what may be in dispute in negotiations.

It is disconcerting to me to hear things like "Tennessee law is an offshoot of the Florida law." Reality is that the Tennessee law is a greater abomination than the Florida law is. It holds out a great deal of hope for people under the guise of collective bargaining, but it really doesn't bother with collective bargaining. It also institutionalizes management control of the bargaining units and institutionalizes the establishment of company unionism.

I also want to make a distinction between secrecy and privacy: I keep hearing that there is a need for secrecy in negotiations and that no one can know what the issues are that are being negotiated over. That is a far cry from the truth, even though in some places it does take place. Responsible unions constantly report to their constituency, members, about what's going on in negotiations, and how it will affect them. And employers, board of education spokemen, public relations people, commonly refer to those same things in news releases to their own constituencies.

Harold Newman: It is fortuituous that Bob Bates raised the question because I was going to raise the same question. I've been bothered by the word *secrecy*. It's an unpleasant word. We may possibly be overreaching. Nobody suggests that the mediator in a steel dispute be entertaining reporters or the parties in the dispute. Yet, your lives, insofar as economics are concerned, are affected as much by the agreement between U.S. Steel and the steelworkers as by any agreement made by the teachers and the board of education in your hometown. And no mediator can function in private, if he doesn't have the confidence of the parties. In every situation, the parties have certain needs that take priority over other needs. If the mediator is in a position where he has the confidence of the parties, and one party says, "Yes, we can come down from asking 4 percent to 3 percent if the other side can do something about Blue Cross coverage"; and if the mediator runs off at the mouth to the other side and says, "Hey, they'll come down to 3 percent," he's dead. He's broken his stick. He has to be able to say to the other side, "I'll lean on them and get them to come down to 3 percent if you can do something for me on the Blue Cross." That's the way mediators work. Can they do that in "sunshine"? Can they do that talking to reporters? Is it any more sinful to do that in the public sector than in the private sector? I submit again there are many private sector negotiations involving utilities, steel, that affect our lives more strongly—economically—than public sector negotiations.

As far as recognizing the public as "those who come and who care," I have a concern that I think Happy Fernandez was articulating. I'm afraid that is a dangerous game to play. Let's use factfinding as an example. When the Taylor committee, which was made up of five very distinguished labor relations professionals, blueprinted the law under which we work in New York State, their report to the governor said that a published factfinding report would act as some kind of catalytic agent. The public would say, "This fine, objective gentleman with his twenty-five years experience has taken sworn testimony of witnesses, examined the data, done a regression analysis on the statistics, and has come up with these recommendations." Then the public will say, "O.K. teachers, O.K. board, why don't you support this factfinding report?" It turned out to be fiction. We send out the factfinding reports. Every day in the week my office pumps factfinding reports out to those citizens out there, and we get as response almost nothing.

Ellen Ainsworth: I have a feeling we are living in different worlds, Mr. Newman. You are telling me the facts are there and that every union keeps its employees informed. I'm neither union nor management but work with community groups all over the state of California. When there is a strike, a hot line goes in. Who do you think is the heaviest user of the hot line for information on budgets, on status of negotiation? It is often the teachers. I think Ralph Flynn will bear me out in this: in half the strikes in California, the facts aren't known. The right to that kind of information is what the public wants, the teachers want, and the school boards all want. Isn't that clear?

John Ryan (Philadelphia Federation of Teachers): To pick up on a point made earlier, certainly the final control of who is going to make the contract decision should be subjected to a ballot. But you do have to look at how democratic this system is and ask if you can really hope for open covenants, totally openly arrived at. Or do you have open covenants for which, at times, you might have to have some privacy? In many negotiations, the more complex and the more critical, there has to be the opportunity for privacy on some occasion for a period of time.

Donald Magruder: You are missing the point of the fact of secrecy in bargaining: It doesn't make any difference if the deal is cut illegally. The point is that negotiations are open all along, and the negotiators are sitting at a table, being observed by members of the public. So the public can get back to the board and let them know what they expect them to do. Even if they cut the deal in private, it doesn't keep that telephone from ringing. So whether you cut the deal in secrecy or not isn't the major issue. The communications with the public are still taking place.

IV.

Parent Participation in Collective Bargaining: Rochester, New York

It is not overly simplistic to say that open meetings laws and sunshine laws are a result of general dissatisfaction and distrust of government institutions, but it is overly simplistic to say that that is the sole reason for Rochester's policy on collective bargaining.

In Rochester, there is a tradition, albeit short, of community groups organized outside the political process having influence on the political system. The board of education, since 1971, before the open meetings law, has allowed the public and press to be present for executive and study sessions. During this period, the change from partisan to nonpartisan status of the board of education possibly supplied further impetus for this open-door direction. Concurrently, the fading local political ward organizations gave way to the rise of neighborhood and community organizations, which began to provide the kinds of services formerly provided by those political bodies. These factors coupled with stands taken by statewide and national public interest groups have created an inviting climate for parent involvement in Rochester.

From the early 1970s the board of education has cooperated with various community groups, such as the Community Schools Council, Rochester Council of Parent Teacher Associations, Bilingual Education Council, and Parents Advisory Council. Negotiated agreements were entered into with two of the above organizations. Community Schools Councils are found in ten schools receiving or eligible for Title I funds. The Bilingual Education Council was formed by parents seeking a voice in the selection of employees in the bilingual program. In 1971 the Parents Advisory Council was brought into existence in an effort to promote voluntary integration and was composed primarily of parents falling into none of the preceeding groups. (Of course, Rochester had its advisory committees mandated by law, such as those for Title I, and the model cities program.)

Working with these groups and others led to the recognition of the need to formalize parent involvement districtwide. This formalization effort resulted in the 1976 adoption of the board of education's Parent Involvement Policy, a document delineating those areas where parents may participate in the educational decision-making process. Among the areas listed were capital and operating budget, instruction, discipline, grading, building utilization, special education, and special services. It is not surprising, having come this far, that the Rochester community would also address the area of collective bargaining in that policy:

Prior to presentation to the Board of Education, Parent Leadership shall have the opportunity to help develop the District's position in collective bargaining with its employees through meeting(s) with the Board's negotiator and members of the negotiating team before the package is developed. Parent Leadership shall have the opportunity to meet regularly with the negotiator and/or members of the negotiating team throughout the negotiations process to be kept informed of progress and to provide parental input.

The Superintendent shall designate a parent representative as part of the District negotiating team. The representative shall be chosen from a list of at least six persons submitted by the Parent Leadership to the Superintendent no later than October 15 of the year preceding contract negotiations. This representative shall, as a member of the District's team, abide by all the guidelines set for members of the team. Caucuses of the District's team shall be restricted to its members as appointed pursuant to contract by the Board and Superintendent.

The document defines Parent Leadership as follows:

At the District level, parent representatives from at least one of the following groups shall have input into decisions: Bilingual Education Council, Community School Council, Parent Advisory Council, District Advisory Council, District Advisory Council to Title I, or Parent Teacher Association. (The heads of these groups are known as Parent Leadership.)

Involvement in collective bargaining was not an issue in and of itself but rather a part of the broader scheme to meet community demands for participation at all levels of educational decision making. Parent advocates of the Parent Involvement Policy focused on section 5 only when other demands were blocked: for example, the selection of principals by the community. This proposal met with board and administrative opposition but eventually survived in its present form, due in part to the willingness of the district's negotiator to "live with" the situation and an absence of strong resistance from the board of education.

The question of the legality of a parent's presence at bargaining was, in effect, circumvented. The current teachers' contract allows either party to have consultants, competent professional or lay representatives, during negotiations. The question of parent representation has therefore not been raised by the teachers' union.

Before you conclude that a parents' utopia exists in upstate New York, let me hasten to say "It just ain't so." Many structures are in place to allow parent participation, but those structures are not always utilized effectively or significantly, and any lack of success may be attributed in varying degrees to administrators, board members, and parents.

Bargaining in the Rochester City School District predates the Taylor Law. Since 1965 the board of education has negotiated with its teachers. Currently, there are four major bargaining units in the district and one small unit of career skills teachers of adults. Also there is a petition before the New York State Public Employment Relations Board (PERB) for recognition of a per diem substitute unit.

The major bargaining units are the Rochester Teachers Association with approximately twenty-three hundred members; the Administrative-Supervisory unit with roughly three hundred twenty-five members, including principals, vice principals, deans, and department heads; the Teachers Aides Association of Rochester, which has about four hundred fifty members; and a fifteen-hundred-member unit of nonteaching personnel, the Board of Education Non-Teaching Employees (BENTE), which is an AFSCME local. With the exception of BENTE, these units fall under the umbrella of the Rochester Teachers Association and are affiliated with the New York State United Teachers (NYSUT). Grouping teachers with administrators makes for a most interesting situation. In a city school district with thirty-eight thousand pupils and approximately sixty building locations, there are only thirty administrators exempted from bargaining. This certainly provides an imbalance of power from a parent perspective.

Nineteen seventy-seven saw a new ingredient added to the mix—the parent. In keeping with the Parent Involvement Policy, parent leaders around the district convened in September 1977 and began compiling the list of six names to submit to the superintendent of schools. In conjunction with the city school district and the Rochester Teachers Association, the Urban League of Rochester sponsored a workshop to acquaint interested parents with collective bargaining. Eric Lawson, regional director for the Public Employment Relations Board (PERB) in western New York, gave an overview of the process and discussed the Taylor Law. Adam Kaufman, counsel and negotiator for the city school district, and David O'Keefe, executive director for the Rochester Teachers Association, described the history of bargaining in Rochester, giving details about negotiations in 1975. Parent leaders, after an interview and screening procedure, submitted six names to the superintendent, and I was selected from that list to serve as the parent representative to the negotiating team.

The issue of how representative I am and whom I represent is not one that can be addressed in absolutes. At no time have I purported to be the voice of all parents in the Rochester City School District; however, I have attempted to achieve a cross section of community opinion by using a network of parent contacts. The composition of that network will be described later.

On October 20, 1977, the superintendent of schools announced my appointment, and the first internal meeting for the district's negotiating team was scheduled for October 21. Twenty-four hours is hardly enough time to prepare, although the old saying "ignorance is bliss" was most applicable as I attended that first team meeting confident of learning whatever would prove necessary. The other members of the negotiating team were the counsel and chief negotiator for the district, Adam Kaufman, and eight top administrators representing major departments in the district: budget, special education, instruction, elementary and secondary administration, personnel, and compensatory education.

The October 21 meeting began the prebargaining stage, which was to last three months. During this period the negotiating team met nine times to consider the contract section by section and make modifications and deletions where it was deemed necessary or prudent. In addition to meeting with the team, I also met frequently with leaders and representatives of the six major parent groups in the district: Community Schools Council, District Advisory Committee to Title I, Rochester Council of Parent Teacher Associations, Parents Advisory Council, Bilingual Education Council, and the Pre-School Parents Council. This core group constituted a fairly representative cross section of parents, which I refer to as Parent Leadership even though more than six parent leaders were involved. No interested parties were excluded from the group, but people were encouraged to attend regularly, in order to avoid spending valuable time bringing truants up to date.

Prebargaining was the only period when a degree of confidentiality was maintained. When meeting with parents, I would indicate the main areas of the contract being addressed and solicit parent responses and opinions to be taken back to the other team members. One such meeting included the district's negotiator so he could hear parent concerns firsthand.

Two proposals in the district's package have been termed "parent proposals" because they are additions obviously included at my request, which I based on needs expressed by many parents. The proposals ask for a commitment from teachers to parent involvement and the establishment of a joint committee, composed of teachers, parents, and administrators, to study the feasibility of parent input in teacher evaluation.

Once the negotiating team had completed the package of initial positions, these were presented to the board of education. The presentations were accomplished during the month of January, with no significant changes by the board.

Packages were exchanged with the union on February 1, 1978, and there was a scurry to see which side could schedule the earlier press conference. All proposals were public information; copies were made available to parents, community groups, and the news media. The first bargaining session was scheduled, at the union's request, for February 28, 1978.

The exchange and public release of proposals increased community interest and therefore increased the amount of time I felt obliged to be in contact with parents. Five Saturday mornings in the months of February and March were designated for meetings with the expanded parent leadership group. The initial purpose of these meetings was for Adam Kaufman and me to explain the district's position and to give our interpretation of the union's demands. It was soon evident, and certainly not unexpected, that most parents in the group were unfamiliar with bargaining in general and knew little about the history of the existing contract, its advantages and disadvantages, or how it compared to contracts outside Rochester. Copies of the contract were made available to parents, and much time was spent on these issues. Adam Kaufman's presence was invaluable, in fact essential, for this exchange of information to occur. The Saturday meetings were also used for negotiations updates.

Parent Leadership invited the union negotiating committee to provide similar insight, but the invitation was declined with the explanation that such an attempt was premature and might be more productive further into bargaining. This meeting has not yet materialized.

Taking place at the same time was the city school district's spring ritual, the budget process, which is a public procedure involving parents and community people and union representatives. On April 15, 1978, the board of education passed a tentative budget allocating monies for contract settlements. The monies were not of the magnitude desired by the unions; but at least there was something in place, and everyone knew it. There was no immediate economic offer made at the bargaining table.

Things moved rather slowly in bargaining through March, April, and the first days of May. The union and district negotiating committees met six times. There was great difficulty in arranging meetings because of the number of meetings (roughly eighteen) already planned for the Budget Advisory Committee, which involved many of the same people. This type of difficulty would again be encountered in later May and June with the closing of school and an unforeseen budget crisis. Proposals and counterproposals were made, but progress was negligible. The district did not offer money, and the union appeared unwilling to move until there was some indication of the district's intention concerning the economic items.

The ides of May brought an event that would restructure negotiations, the Waldert decision. The Waldert tax case was to become a household phrase across the city. In that case, the Court of Appeals supported a decision that it was unconstitutional for the city of Rochester (as well as Buffalo and fifty-six other school districts and cities) to continue taxing beyond its 2 percent constitutional limit to finance retirement and social security benefits for city employees, a practice that had been allowed for several years under special state legislation. The city and city school district were forced to cut their budgets by $32 million. By June 1978, after passage of a variety of local laws, including a number of user fees, the board of education was forced to trim its budget in excess of $6 million. Included in that $6 million were the monies previously allocated for contract settlements.

In the three bargaining sessions that occurred between mid-May and June 30, 1978, the union's position became very clear. They would not or could not negotiate until money was available. The board of education refused to make further cuts in programs. Hence, on July 6, impasse was declared, and both sides awaited the appointment of a mediator.

PERB-appointed mediator Howard Foster scheduled the first mediation session for July 31. This lasted twelve hours. Two more such sessions were to follow in August. There was some movement by both sides but not sufficient to avoid a twelve-hour factfinding hearing on September 15. We are now awaiting the fact finder's report. Since each side presented briefs of more than four hundred pages, Howard Foster may never emerge from under this mound of papers.

Many of the bargaining and mediation sessions did not include the entire teams. It was suggested in May that only the negotiators meet. This arrangement was unacceptable to Adam Kaufman and me since it was understood that either I was included at all times or I would not serve on the team. Therefore, the sessions included the negotiator for the teachers, the chairperson for the union negotiating committee, Adam Kaufman, and myself. The members of this smaller group would meet, exchange proposals, talk, and then return to their respective teams for caucuses. This format was also used for two of the three mediation sessions.

Throughout this phase, Adam Kaufman and I continued to meet with Parent Leadership and discuss the status of bargaining. Copies of the proposals and counterproposals that had been exchanged were duplicated and distributed. The parents were equally, if not better, informed than the board of education.

There were several contract issues of interest to parents: parent-teacher reports, parent-teacher conferences, teaching hours, discipline of students, and evaluation of teachers. The Rochester Teachers Association has proposals in three of these areas that are not at all satisfactory to parents. Before the financial crisis resulting from the Waldert decision, the economic items in the contract were not the first priority of parents in the community. Salaries and benefits affect us as taxpayers but have become a focal point only since the board of education was forced to take a no-raise position and the president of the teachers' union stated that teachers will strike if no money is forthcoming. Before the Waldert decision, parents and the community were willing to accept the board's budget allocation for salary increments.

Of necessity, my next remarks will be confined to the experience in Rochester and to this particular round of bargaining. Some of the comments may sound naïve, and some probably are; but to my knowledge this is the first time an outsider has watched and fully participated in what some people believe to be a quasi-mystical process. I hope this lack of sophistication will not diminish the value of my perceptions.

Because of the very nature of the negotiations process, parent involvement can be easily impeded and the parent participant excluded. The Rochester experience is otherwise. It is fair to say that I have been intimately involved with every aspect of this round of bargaining and, as a result, may be more aware of what has happened in negotiations than even other members of the district's team. This situation arose when the bargaining and mediation sessions were limited to the negotiators and one member of each team. I was always the representative from the district's team to accompany Adam Kaufman. In some respects, this may have caused internal problems. Some members may have felt excluded, which increased the pressure on the two of us to update and inform those members. The exclusion of the entire team, however, possibly allowed the negotiator to influence compromise that might not have occurred otherwise.

A second aspect of involvement was my presence at all closed sessions of the board of education at which the subject of bargaining was discussed. There appeared to be a keen awareness on the part of board members that their performance was being observed. Whether that awareness will result in more responsive, responsible decision making is unclear; it is simply too early to tell. I am told, however, that the board did less negotiating with its negotiator and team than in the past and attempted to deal with the issues on a substantive basis.

It has not been my experience that heat generated at the bargaining table caused school administrators to be more susceptible to union proposals. If anything, the administrators I have witnessed became more rigid. In Rochester, the board of education is not at the table and somewhat removed from the pressure of bargaining. They are, however, exposed to the public rumblings of the union and, because of what I view as the inherent nature of school boards, are more susceptible to union demands.

My perceptions of the union negotiating committee are based on the negotiator, the committee chairperson, and the president. They are the only people with whom I have talked to any extent. A NYSUT field representative is spokesperson for the union. I am inclined to think his not being a member of the bargaining unit occasionally thwarts attempts to move the union team toward compromise. Whether by design or not, he seems unable to assess what is palatable to his team and cannot contradict or overcome the individual positions of the chairperson of the team. He has made it quite clear that the union is unwilling to bargain with parents, and the specific proposals dealing with parent involvement and teacher evaluation were not welcomed with open arms.

The structure of parent participation in collective bargaining in itself is not as important as the commitment of the board of education and the administration to its success. Probably the key person in implementing any form of participation is the negotiator. Adam Kaufman, the district's counsel and negotiator, has shown a great commitment. His acceptance of me as an equal team member set the tone for my acceptance as such by others involved. His willingness to meet and talk at length with parents about negotiations has been the basis for the education of parents and the community in collective bargaining.

Working with Adam Kaufman has convinced me of the advantage of having someone within the system serve as the negotiator. Not only does he administer the contract, but also he must live and work with all people involved once bargaining has ended. The fact that Adam Kaufman is a city resident with a child in the city school system adds to his credibility in the community.

An important byproduct of this particular form of parent participation has been the increased dialogue between parents and the district administration. This dialogue might not have been as extensive and informal under other structures, such as sunshine bargaining, third-party bargaining, or parent-mediators. Although parents have not and most likely will not always agree with the district, there is now greater empathy out there for the mode of the board of education's operations, particularly in relation to bargaining.

A final analysis of the Rochester experiment is impossible since we are still bargaining. But I do feel safe in stating that participation on the employer's bargaining team requires not only cooperation but also commitment from the employer. There need be only a few key people committed, but those few are absolutely essential. Therefore, only districts with similar histories of attempted government openness and citizen involvement will achieve any degree of success with this form of public access.

V.

A Teacher Perspective on School Governance and Collective Bargaining

John E. Dunlop

The question of whether collective bargaining has blunted the influence of various publics on the educational enterprise touches some complex and perplexing problems—complex because there is a diversity, structural and philosophical, in the ways school systems are operated in this country; perplexing because the question involves problems fundamental to the operation of our government.

The process of locating the primary motivating force behind demands for greater public access to the bargaining process raises all the complicated and perplexing problems inherent in the public access issue and permits us to make an initial macrocosmic overview of it.

There is no one motivating force behind any demand for greater public access to the bargaining process. Any such demand is the product of several forces at work in our society and, specifically, in the governance of education. Today, there is a pervasive mistrust of government caused by the failure of liberal programs to solve intractable social problems, our experience in Vietnam, Watergate, and venal politicians. The simple fact is that schools are government enterprises, and therefore the pervasive mistrust of government applies to the schools. Coupled with public mistrust has been the rise in democratic participation in all aspects of government. Previously excluded, neglected, or disenfranchised groups have mobilized, appointed spokespersons, and sought a voice in government decision making. Teacher organizations are part of this movement, as are blacks and other racial and ethnic minorities, women, and consumers. The wave of participatory democracy has not passed. Other groups are forming and following in the path of the activist groups of the 1960s and early 1970s. In education, groups of parents are demanding a greater voice in educational decision making, a voice previously denied them by traditional values and processes.

Partly as a result of a general mistrust of government and a rise in participatory democracy, there has been a shift of policy leadership from executives to legislatures; this is evident on the national scene where President Carter is having trouble getting Congress to pass his programs relatively intact. This shift has particular import for the operation of schools, because school operations, from policy making to policy implementation, have been traditionally dominated by the chief executive officer, the superintendent.

Such a shift has been hastened by the decline in the acceptance of the neutral competence theory of management. The neutral competence theory holds that administrators of government operations are hired for their technical expertise and work according to explicit, objective standards rather than for partisan or political reasons. Professionalism, efficiency, and effectiveness are the primary watchwords. This theory was widely accepted in education. The current accepted theory holds that government administration, including the formulation of policy, is part of the political process and cannot be practically separated from it.

Traditionally, the American public has given enthusiastic support of public education. Today, however, this support is being severely shaken. With reports of functional illiterates graduating, test scores declining, discipline failing, and costs increasing, the public faith in education is not what it once was. Despite the traditional support of public education, the general public has never really understood how the educational enterprise has operated, particularly the role played by its representative agency, the school board. A 1975 National School Board Association report stated:

The national picture reveals that the people neither understood the functions of school boards nor believe that they should have most of the legal responsibilities which they now do have. But the national picture also suggests that these opinions are not deeply held and probably result more from ignorance than from deep conviction. This is a volatile situation. It seems that public opinion easily can be swayed by anyone who, for whatever motives, wishes to change the present system of governance.[1]

As for school boards themselves, they have to a great extent encouraged and fostered the present state of public confusion as to their role and function. School board members have not been selected for their

---

1. National School Board Association, *The People Look at Their School Boards* (Evanston, Ill.: National School Board Association, 1975).

political leadership qualities nor for any stand they may have taken on school issues but rather for their capacity to avoid any controversy and their ability to project an image of altruistic concern for education. Nonpolitical control has been their guiding principle. Once elected, they have acted at the trustee end of the representation spectrum, seldom the delegate end. In an age of rising democratic participation, institutional mechanisms, such as school boards, that have developed set patterns of operating may not be flexible enough to adapt to changing values and processes.

Traditionally, superintendents and their administrative staffs have traditionally been the dominant element in the local educational enterprise. School boards have deferred to the superintendent. As one commentator has said, school boards have not governed but merely legitimated the policy recommendations of the superintendent, thus reducing democratic control of education to "little more than a sham." This has been due primarily to the neutral competence theory of management and the desire to keep political controversy out of school operations. In an enterprise dependent upon technical expertise, decision makers turn to the technicians. But if the technicians do not provide solutions to technical problems, one does not really need technicians, or at least one is more comfortable in ignoring their advice. All educational professionals are suspect today; administrators, teachers, and the decision makers may be deferring to them less and less.

Teachers traditionally have been a relatively silent group. In recent years, however, owing to a general rise in group identity and group activism, they have asserted themselves more often and with greater vehemence. Collective bargaining is, in part, an institutionalization of their group identity and activism.

The interplay between changes in public attitudes about government in general and changes in the operation of government itself and the ways schools have operated in the past are really the root causes of any demand for greater public access to the bargaining process. The bargaining process itself, however, tends to accelerate any such demand because one fundamental problem confronting legislative policy makers considering any aspect of the collective bargaining process remains unresolved. This unresolved problem has plagued public sector bargaining since its inception. At the risk of dredging up a seemingly dead and buried concept, let us call it the sovereignty problem.

The sovereignty argument was originally raised to block public sector employee organizations from being recognized and allowed to bargain with government agencies. The argument held that the "supreme, absolute, and uncontrollable power by which any independent state is governed" ultimately reposes, in our system of government, in the people, and that to accord any organization a position from which that organization could interfere in the business of the sovereign's representatives would be intolerable. The sovereignty argument, however, did not prevent many states from adopting teacher collective bargaining statutes. Its rhetoric was archaic, and it offered no practical guidance to policy makers facing active and cohesive employee groups. State legislatures dismissed the sovereignty argument in part by saying in effect that it did not bar legislatures from authorizing government agencies from entering into collective bargaining relationships with their employees. But a residue of the sovereignty argument remained and has continually been raised in a wide variety of policy issues in public sector collective bargaining. It holds that even though a government may bargain with its employees on the terms and conditions of government employment, there is a limit to which the employee can coerce the government into doing anything. Most state legislatures passing collective bargaining laws have limited the capacity of employees to coerce by outlawing the right to strike. Even in states that allow the right to strike, such as Pennsylvania and Hawaii, limits on coercive capacity were drawn on standards of public welfare and safety. In addition, many state legislatures place specific limits on the topics that could be bargained, thereby attempting to limit the coercive capacity of employee groups to certain specified subjects.

But to some observers of the public sector bargaining scene such limits are only cosmetic and fail to touch the core problem of sovereignty. These observers are troubled by what they perceive to be contradictions in a government system that says the people are sovereign and then allows, in their estimation, privileges in government decision making to a favored few. To these observers, the rising activism of public sector employee organizations in the political arena, as opposed to the collective bargaining arena, compounds the threat to popular sovereignty. Harry H. Wellington and Ralph K. Winter put this view best:

The trouble is that if [public sector] unions are able to withhold labor—to strike—as well as employ the usual methods of political pressure, they may possess a disproportionate share of effective power in the process of decision. Collective bargaining would then be so effective a pressure as to skew the results of the normal American political process.[2]

Although the sovereignty problem may be the most difficult philosophical conundrum for policy makers to solve, it may be, given the

---

2. Harry H. Wellington and Ralph K. Winter, *The Unions and the Cities* (Washington, D.C.: Brookings Institution, 1971), p. 25.

deep current of pragmatism that runs through the American body public, that the basic concern manifested by any demand for access is really very simple. The general public may be saying that if they are expected to bear the brunt of the disruption of public services, they should be apprised of the dimensions of the dispute long before chaos descends upon them, and that public access to the bargaining process will give them such timely apprisal.

With all this as background, let us now consider some of the specific questions put before this conference.

Disproportionate Economic Power?

Is it indeed the case that under collective bargaining a teacher union tends to become a dominant political and economic power in the formulation of educational policy and allocation of scarce resources, outmuscling parent groups, taxpayer organizations, and chambers of commerce? More than twelve years of teacher collective bargaining have demonstrated that political and economic dominance, or more accurately the appearance of dominance, turns on variables other than exclusive recognition and the right to bargain hours, wages, and working conditions. Such dominance, if it exists at all for more than a fleeting moment, comes not from the existence of bargaining but from organizational solidarity and cohesion and the political and economic environment the organization operates in. To these factors must be added the nature of the educational enterprise and its traditional ways of operating.

Teacher organizations twelve to thirteen years ago had a greater potential for such dominance than they do today. That potential had less to do with bargaining than with the general economic climate, the public esteem with which education was held, and the deference shown by the public and its representatives to the wisdom of educational experts. Today, the potential for dominance is limited because inflation is rampant and taxpayers are not acquiescent. Education is seen as failing, and the experts are in dispute. In a recent Gallup poll on public confidence in education, 38 percent of the people polled gave the schools an A or B rating. In 1974, 48 percent gave the schools A or B ratings. Conversely, in 1978, 19 percent gave the schools a D or failing rating, while only 11 percent gave such ratings in 1974.

As for the allocation of resources, insiders, whether they be the superintendent, the administrative staff, or a teachers' organization, may enjoy a positional advantage. This positional advantage is increased the more the operation relies upon technical expertise. L. Harmon Zeigler noted this in an article reviewing school board research:

If schools are really service organizations, providing professional expertise to a specialized population, then we can assume that the specialized [population] does not know what will best serve its interests and must rely on professional judgement.[3]

Again, however, the positional advantage is maintained only so long as the experts and their programs are credible.

It can be argued that at the most fundamental level, teacher collective bargaining was a revolution within the ranks of the experts, a revolution to determine which group of experts would have what share in policy making. It did not contemplate a change in the way the educational enterprise was going to be run because it assumed it would be run as before. Changes were occurring in the body politic, however, separate and distinct from, although affecting, the professional revolution. These changes were altering traditional values and perceptions about how the educational enterprise ought to be run and raised to the level of recognition and debate contradictions and unresolved problems already present in the system of educational governance.

Undue Pressure during Bargaining?

The question of whether the heat generated at the bargaining table causes public representatives to lose sight of public interest presumes a level of public input in the operation of education that has never existed. It presumes the public will was always clearly manifested and carefully considered by school officials in the days before collective bargaining. All thoughtful observers of educational governance have concluded this has never been the case. L. Harmon Zeigler states:

At the risk of generalizing from somewhat shaky data, I suggest that school board members are more likely than other elected officials—to reject the notion of responding to demands and to accept the fundamental tenets of a service organization. One must do what is best for the clients, whether or not they understand what their actual interests are.[4]

He then adds a rhetorical question: "Why do school boards represent the views of the superintendent to the public, rather than representing the views of the public to the superintendent?"

One of the great ironies may be that the bargaining process cast before the public, for the first time, issues for the public to decide. The fact is that in the heat of some collective bargaining situations the two contending parties, the board-administration on the one hand and the

---

3. L. Harmon Zeigler, "School Board Research: The Problems and the Prospects," in *Understanding School Boards*, ed. Peter J. Cistone (Lexington, Mass.: D. C. Heath and Co.), p. 4.
    4. Ibid., p. 6.

teachers on the other, have turned to the public as the final arbiter of the issues in dispute and, in the process, may have closed one era of educational governance and opened another.

The example some observers cite to prove the contention that the public will be given short shrift in teacher bargaining because public administrators are scared witless in face of the power of teacher unions is the New York City teachers bargaining experiences of the 1960s and early 1970s. The conventional wisdom holds that the teachers' union clubbed the city administrators into accepting outrageous union demands because these public officials wanted settlement at any cost to avoid the disruption of essential services. To these observers the proof of this was the subsequent fiscal crisis of the city. But to one labor relations commentator that, in fact, was not the case. Joan Weitzman sees other causes for the crisis:

While New York City's problem stems in part from fiscal mismanagement, incompetent officials, political shenanigans, and certain aspects of the city's labor relations program, it is also true that such factors as the national recession, inflation, and the energy crisis have impacted severely on New York City and would probably have caused financial trauma even without the presence of a highly unionized government work force.[5]

To place at the bargaining tables public representatives other than, or in addition to, those public representatives already charged with the responsibility to represent the public does not solve or eliminate the problems of fiscal mismanagement, incompetent officials, political shenanigans; nor does it change the facts of economic life.

Union-Government Collusion?

Is the political power of public sector unions such that they can get their friends elected to public office, therefore ensuring a more sympathetic hearing of their proposals by public officials? This question raises the issue commented on by Wellington and Winter. Their thesis is that the coercive capacity of public sector unions and their ability to intrude in the selection of public representatives wrenches our system of government out of all proper proportion.

I would agree with this thesis if, in fact, public sector unions had unlimited coercive capabilities and could, in fact, elect officials that were mere union puppets. Nowhere does a public union have unlimited coercive capabilities. Aside from the limits that may exist in the law, such as strike bans or heavy fines for illegal strikes or limits on the

---

5. Joan P. Weitzman, "The Effect of Economic Restraints on Public-Sector Collective Bargaining: The Lessons of New York City," *Employee Relations Law Journal* 2, no. 3 (winter 1977): 286.

topics of bargaining, public sector unions are limited directly by public attitudes and public desires. It is a matter of survival, not only for the union but for the public employees as job holders. A public-be-damned attitude by a public sector union would be suicidal. Simply put, there are systemic limits on the coercive capabilities of public sector unions; the most important and effective are not found in any bargaining law.

In addition, there are systemic limits on the ability of public sector unions to elect public officials tied unequivocally to these unions. No one can seriously imagine any relatively competent public official declaring "Yes, I am for the teachers' union, and I will do whatever it tells me to." But a public official need not say it to become a target of public opprobrium. The public will react if his or her actions in policy making smack of collusion with a public sector union, and such reactions will be manifested in elections, council meetings, and the press.

The system currently possesses the mechanisms capable of adjusting any unfavorable power balance. Implicit in the question of union-elected officials is the suggestion that current mechanisms of representation may not be fulfilling their functions and therefore new mechanisms must be created. If this suggestion is in fact true, and it is doubtful, then the solution lies not with the fine tuning of one facet of educational decision making, collective bargaining, but with an overhaul of the whole mechanism of educational policy making. This overhaul must include the selection and role of the school board member and the selection and role of the chief executive officer, not simply a decision about whether additional public representatives should be present during or participate in bargaining.

Where Do Parent and Teacher Interests Differ?
The interests of the teachers and parent-citizens differ on any matter that involves money. Whenever scarce resources are to be allocated, whenever one group—say taxpayers—gives up some resources to pay another group—say school teachers—conflict exists. This symposium should not investigate where teachers and parent-citizens differ but whether their differences can be resolved with the governmental mechanisms currently in place in a manner that promotes the public welfare.

Does the School Board Truly Represent Public Views?
The classic quandary of a representative democracy is, Who speaks for whom? Hobbes, Rousseau, Burke, and others have reflected on the problem of representation. Such a theoretical question is purely speculative unless one concludes that the current structure and representation mechanisms have failed completely. If one does not so conclude, then he

or she must address the additional question, Should we add representative group upon representative group, thus compounding representation and possibly creating useless conflict among different public representatives?

Is Citizen Participation Inconsistent with the Intent of the Law?

To answer whether or not citizen participation in negotiations violates the intent of collective bargaining legislation, the exact dimensions of citizen participation must be defined. If participation is merely sitting and listening, the answer is no, it is not inconsistent with the intent of collective bargaining legislation. It may not be strategically wise, given the dynamics of bargaining, but it would not violate any specific legislative intent. But, if participation means the right to discuss, to make proposals and counterproposals, it would be inconsistent with the intent of collective bargaining legislation. It would be inconsistent because all state collective bargaining laws clearly designate two specific parties to the bargaining. All such laws require good-faith bargaining. To have an active third party violates the two-party concept. To have a third party capable of vetoing a negotiated contract violates the good-faith concept, not to mention the fact that a skillful employer could avoid bargaining altogether under such circumstances. Tripartite bargaining could create the instability and disharmony in the operation of a public agency's labor relations that bargaining statutes are designed to overcome.

What Form Citizen Involvement?

Citizen-parent involvement is in order, but the form of such involvement cannot be discussed solely in the context of teacher collective bargaining. Citizen-parent involvement can only be discussed in reference to current institutions of representation in school governance, with recognition of realities in our democracy that jars some cherished myths.

A school board is the institution in school governance designed to represent the citizen-parents. If it does not, the fault does not lie with the institution per se but with the fact that no one has ever expected or wanted its members to fulfill their representative roles. The question then is, Is the institution so weighted with failure it cannot be redeemed? Or alternatively, have we really come to the conclusion that we want greater democratic participation in the operation of our schools?

As for specific suggestions of what form citizen-parent involvement should take, it should be assumed that school boards will continue to exist and will be the representatives of the citizen-parents. Nothing prevents public discussion of the parties' initial proposals under current bargaining practices. It is usually not done because the parties wish to be free of initial public pressure that may prematurely freeze one or both of the parties in positions. To mandate a public discussion of initial proposals politicizes the bargaining too soon. If anything is brought to the public it should be the relatively well-settled and matured positions of the parties after all the inflated aspects have been winnowed out. This is the very concept underlying the publication of fact finders' reports required in most state bargaining statutes. As for attendance at the bargaining table, the public is at the bargaining table in the form of their board and staff representatives. To increase the number of people present will inevitably fragment the bargaining process to such an extent that real, honest interchanges, proposals, and counterproposals may be very difficult.

When it comes to public participation beyond the school board and administration, definitely no. Nothing but chaos will result. The nominal representatives of the public, the school board and administrative staff, can easily defer to the other representatives and not do anything in bargaining. Those most capable of making judgments on myriad administrative matters entailed in collective bargaining agreements will be silent. For bargaining to work, both parties must have the willingness and freedom to make proposals and counterproposals, and more important, they must feel free to discuss all matters fully. If either party is inhibited, bargaining will not take place.

Nothing in current teacher bargaining, however, prevents citizen-parents playing a role as mediators or third parties in impasse resolution, and in some instances, as members of specially appointed blue-ribbon panels, they have done so.

The right to vote on final terms already exists in some states, especially on economic matters. Although it may be seen as the ultimate answer to the sovereignty issue, it can do great harm to good-faith collective bargaining. The separation between the school board bargainers and their constituents is too great to allow for the kind of interchange necessary to explain why certain decisions were made to reach agreement. The bargaining process is, in large measure, an amending of aspirations, and for one to accept the amendments one must know and feel the problems confronting the decision maker. The public cannot possibly know and feel the problems confronting its representatives over the full range of bargaining issues.

Finally, any discussion of teacher collective bargaining and the problem of public representation in that bargaining must recognize that the classical concept of democracy—an informed, interested, rational electorate willing to participate in discussion furthering community interests—is a myth. The fact is that most people under our government exhibit little interest in public affairs. Few participate actively. Moreover, some are favored, and some are disadvantaged in government decision making, owing to differences in skill, social class, education, and personality characteristics. No amount of tinkering will eliminate these political facts of life.

Citizen Involvement in Teacher Negotiations: A Caution

Robert P. Bates

The rhetoric emanating from some management sources, the organized right-wing, and some well-meaning but misinformed media persons would have the general public believe that public employee collective bargaining, in general, and teacher collective bargaining, in specific, have taken over public institutions for personal gain, to the detriment of the consumer. Some remedies frequently proposed are to deny collective bargaining rights altogether and, where that is not possible, to restrict the collective bargaining process to wages and benefits only and to reserve all decisions on policies and conditions to management; a variation of this idea calls for letting the sun shine in, opening collective negotiations to the public to provide for citizen participation in the process. But the contention that teacher bargaining has taken over the operation of public instruction is ludicrous. All one has to do to disprove this notion is to sample a few collective bargaining agreements in public education.

Citizens should and do participate in the collective bargaining process in public education. They do so through elected boards, appointed managers, and often professional negotiators hired to represent the public's interest on management's side of the table. Definitions of the key elements, citizens and collective bargaining, should help demonstrate this.

There may be confusion about the term *citizen:* when we refer to the citizen, which citizen are we referring to? Leaders of right-to-work organizations are citizens; leaders of anti–collective bargaining groups are citizens; leaders of the chamber of commerce are citizens; and, indeed, teachers, leaders of the Parent Teacher Association, students, and most people who live in the United States are citizens. Direct participation by any or all of these various interests in the collective bargaining process could at the very best only produce chaos. Well-prepared and well-informed representatives are necessary to properly represent the public's interest in the collective bargaining process.

It is essential to this discussion that we understand what we mean when we refer to *collective bargaining*. In the private sector, collective bargaining laws require that employers meet and negotiate in good faith with representatives of their employees, if a majority of the employees have elected to act collectively, to establish their wages, benefits, and other terms and conditions of employment. While there is no requirement to make concessions, if and when agreement is reached, the pact is expressed in a contract; if ratified by the parties, the contract is binding and effective for the duration set forth in the agreement. If agreement is not reached, employees have the right to strike in an effort to enforce their demands. While this process is imperfect, in the vast majority of circumstances, it works. The need to resort to strike action is minimal.

There is no clear national policy on collective bargaining in the public sector. In its absence, a hodgepodge of public policy has developed: across the country we see the whole spectrum of attitudes toward the bargaining process. At one end, there is the statutory requirement to bargain with a limited right to strike: an example is Pennsylvania. At the opposite end, there is statutory prohibition against engaging in collective bargaining: Missouri is an example. In between, there are jurisdictions where collective bargaining exists in fact without regulatory legislation but with the approval of the judiciary: for instance, Illinois. There are still other places where statutes purport to provide for collective bargaining but in reality are nothing more than meet-and-confer statutes, which only frustrate the employee's expectations of bargaining: the Florida law is illustrative of this.

Public employees who attempt to exercise the right to bargain collectively even where it is supposedly guaranteed by the statutes are frequently threatened with repressive action, including fines and jail. In some areas such as Maryland, if employee organizations exercise the right to strike, they may lose their right to represent. Where the opponents of collective bargaining have been unable to prevent it from becoming public policy or to dilute it beyond recognition, they continue their attack on the process through the demand for legislated penalties. The position of the American Federation of Teachers (AFT) on collective bargaining in the public sector is that the National Labor Relations Act, including its provision of the right to strike, should be extended to cover public employees. It is my view that if there is no ability to strike, or to threaten to strike, there is no collective bargaining.

The atmospheres in which collective bargaining takes place in the various jurisdictions throughout this country are obviously varied. Experiments with collective bargaining in public have been disastrous. In some situations, the public's apathetic response to the opportunity to observe the process rendered it nearly meaningless; however, in some circumstances, what occurred was the development of a carnival atmosphere. The parties tended to be publicly polarized and entrenched in their positions and found themselves unable to reach agreement.

The AFT's perception of the problems in sunshine bargaining is reinforced by a consensus view of mediators questioned by the Federal Mediation and Conciliation Service (FMCS). The overall assessment of mediators having experience with these laws is that "open meetings hamper, or at least delay, bargaining," according to the FMCS Office of Research. Among the findings of the FMCS study were that, in general, the public does not attend, that open bargaining tends to harden and polarize positions thus hampering the process of agreement, and that negotiators put on a show for the public rather than engage in serious bargaining. I know of no better way to produce an atmosphere in which collective bargaining can be frustrated and to ensure that no agreement may be reached than bargaining in public.

The major strategy of the anti–collective bargaining element has been to limit severely the scope of negotiations through attempts to achieve legislative constraints and court action attacking existing collective agreements. The motivating principle behind these efforts is that of sovereignty of the public employer in the making of educational policy. Interestingly enough, this was the same argument initially used to find public sector collective bargaining illegal. Where such efforts are successful, the result is a return to unilateral determination of conditions of employment.

But in order for teacher bargaining to be effective, the scope of bargaining must be as broad as possible. In teacher negotiations, conflict is most likely in the determination of educational policy since these policy issues overlap frequently with working conditions. For example, some management rights advocates would argue that to determine the hours of work in a school day is to set an educational policy and, therefore, not subject to determination through bargaining. This, of course, ignores the rather obvious fact that when and how a person works are conditions of his or her employment. Other such issues are assignment to extra work after the regular workday and assignment of supervisory roles, both without compensation. It may well be that certain employee obligations result from educational policy making. But it is equally true that the obligations resulting from those decisions are conditions of employment that should be determined through the bilateral bargaining process.

Most citizens want meaningful education for children. Educators for the most part have dedicated their lives to this purpose, so in this regard, the two are not adversaries. Citizens who support public schools want the educational policies that are best for children; again, that is not inconsistent with the desires of educators. What must be understood is that acceptable conditions of employment must also be achieved. Collective bargaining advocates in public education and education advocates can certainly satisfy more of their respective needs by working collectively than by falling victim to those who would encourage divisiveness.

Response

Comment by Mary McCormick

The paper by Robert Bates is an able presentation of orthodox assumptions about the collective bargaining process in the public sector and in education in particular; the paper by John Dunlop poses some important questions regarding the nature and structure of collective bargaining in education. Despite their different approaches to the issue, the fundamental point made by both Bates and Dunlop is that the present collective bargaining process is working well.

The satisfaction expressed by these two writers may derive from teacher perceptions that the current collective bargaining structure is functioning well for their needs. Indeed, it may be unfair to expect Bates and Dunlop to adopt a broad, critical perspective of a process that has served their interests so adequately.

That many individuals and groups with an interest in education, either as users of educational services or as providers of revenues, have expressed considerable dissatisfaction with many aspects of public education suggests, however, that the system is not responsive to *their* needs. The demand for public access to the collective bargaining process is an expression of that dissatisfaction and of the difficulty those groups not directly represented at the bargaining table have in affecting collective bargaining outcomes, which are fundamentally political outcomes. The crux of the problem is how to ensure that the collective bargaining process in education, as well as in other public services, is consistent with the requirements of political democracy.

The introduction of collective bargaining to public education highlighted the decision-making process and emphasized the political nature of that process. As Dunlop correctly indicates, education is no longer viewed as an essentially administrative function (the neutral competence theory) but is regarded as having a significant political component. The introduction of collective bargaining guaranteed access to the now visibly political decision-making process for those who deliver educational services—but not necessarily for those who use or pay for those services. Collective bargaining per se does not blunt the influence of various publics, but neither has it been accompanied by widespread recognition that various publics should have input into the collective bargaining process. The uniqueness of collective bargaining in the public sector is not in the characteristics of the employees but in the characteristics of the employer.

Rather than considering the critical implications of these developments and the changes in the collective bargaining process that should be made to accommodate the various publics, Bates and Dunlop focus primarily on the issue of whether there should be collective bargaining in education and whether teachers ought to have the right to strike. I am in agreement with Bates and Dunlop on these issues, but I find a fundamental inconsistency in their arguing for collective bargaining in the public sector and the right to strike for public employees and yet failing to extend the need for reform to other aspects of the collective bargaining process.

Those factors that distinguish municipal employees as more than just one of many competing interest groups in a pluralistic democracy are frequently cited as reasons why collective bargaining and unionized public employees distort the decision-making process. Teachers do occupy a strategic position in the educational process. It is because of their position, however, and the fact that the interests of teachers are often in direct conflict with other interest groups that teachers require the protection of collective bargaining. But providing safeguards to teachers does not mean that other interests should be excluded from the decision-making process.

When collective bargaining was first introduced to the public sector and the strike ban imposed, there was no attempt to distinguish among different types of public services and different types of public employees. If teachers go out on strike, the immediate danger to the community is no greater than that posed by strikes by many private sector employees. Removal of the strike ban for teachers would probably improve the collective bargaining process in education. As recent experience indicates, the ban on strikes is often ineffective as a strike deterrent. Moreover, the "illegality" of strikes appears to put undue pressures on both school boards and unions to achieve labor peace, an outcome that may be inconsistent at the time with other objectives of the school boards, the public, and the teachers.

While Bates and Dunlop readily identify this one area where reform is needed, they dismiss as unimportant, unnecessary, or impractical other changes in the system. Public access is one way of ensuring greater accountability of those who represent various publics. Bates dismisses the question of citizen participation as being redundant since citizens already participate through "elected boards, appointed managers, and often professional negotiators hired to represent the public's interest on management's side of the table." Bates, however, does not consider how the public interest is determined, how well the public interest is represented by schools boards, managers, and professional negotiators, and how effectively these representatives are held accountable by the public under present collective bargaining structures.

In contrast, Dunlop admits that the current system may result in management's being unrepresentative. He quotes Ziegler to the effect that school boards traditionally have represented the opinion of superintendents to the public and not vice versa. He cites no evidence that collective bargaining has changed the situation. But, he goes no further.

Rather, Bates and Dunlop suggest that any changes to increase citizen input into and influence over the collective bargaining process in education would produce undesirable outcomes. The thrust of their defense is that these changes would make the process function less smoothly. Both raise the specter of "chaos" that would be produced by too much citizen participation. What they appear to have forgotten is that no one has ever argued that the democratic decision-making process is the most efficient way to determine the allocation of government resources.

Because of the great diversity in educational systems, a variety of changes are necessary to improve the collective bargaining process. One change that would allow for various groups to have greater influence over the outcomes of the collective bargaining process would be reform of the contract ratification process. Dunlop presents the question of whether school negotiators lose sight of the public interest when they are at the bargaining table because of union pressures and accede to demands they would not accede to ordinarily. That this question was posed with respect to school rather than union negotiators relates to the fact that the bargaining agreement reached by union and school negotiators is almost always final from the school's perspective but may be rejected by the union's rank and file. Because of this, the emphasis of collective bargaining negotiations is more on reaching a settlement that will be acceptable to the union rank and file rather than the various publics. Frequently, the terms of the contract settlement are not made public until long after the contract has been ratified by the union's membership.

A ratification process similar to the union's should be instituted on management's side so that contracts must be reviewed by an elected, representative body (not present at the bargaining table) that has the power to ratify or reject the contract. Public discussion, perhaps in the form of hearings, ought to be required before the ratification vote. This type of change would result in a greater effort to inform the public about the issues to be decided in collective bargaining and increased attention on the part of those who negotiate on behalf of school districts to the interests of various publics. This reform would have the advantage of not increasing the number of direct participants in the bargaining process so that it becomes unwieldy while ensuring that the interests of those not actually sitting at the table are considered in the decision-making process.

Although unions operate under such procedures, Bates and Dunlop have a double standard when considering management's ratification process. Dunlop is very pessimistic regarding reform of ratification procedures and suggests that democratic decision making is not even possible in education. He asserts that citizens can never be educated or informed so they are capable of understanding collective bargaining decisions and outcomes: "The separation between the school board bargainers and their constituents is too great to allow for the kind of interchange necessary to explain why certain decisions were made to reach agreement." Perhaps what Dunlop fears is that different kinds of decisions or outcomes would be reached if school bargainers had to explain the terms of contract settlements to their constituents.

Reform of the ratification process is only one way to permit the public to be informed about and influence the outcomes of the collective bargaining process. What is disturbing is that Bates and Dunlop dismiss all proposals for reform that would increase citizen involvement. The collective bargaining process must be strengthened from both management and union perspectives. While there should be no question that collective bargaining ought to be allowed and that teachers should have the right to strike, there also must be increased public access to the bargaining process, increased public influence over the outcomes of collective bargaining decisions, and a better system for increasing management accountability.

Discussion Highlights

Exploring the conviction in the papers by Dunlop and Bates that the only necessary mechanism for public representation already exists in the form of the school board, the participants identified two possible roles for board members, that of the delegate and that of the trustee, and they speculated about which of these the public should expect board members to assume. Also on the theme of how constituencies should be represented, it was suggested that, at times, citizens acting independently of the school board might become part of the union's constituency. Union-affiliated participants rejected this notion. The group then considered at length the need for mechanisms for public access, short of "sunshine" or third-party bargaining, that would allow increased public information and influence on the outcome of negotiations—*Editor.*

David Seeley (Public Education Association): John, let's just take your assumptions: (1) The myth of democratic governance of education. People really didn't control public education until collective bargaining came along; a group of expert administrators were controlling it. (2) Collective bargaining is primarily a struggle between two groups of experts—would the teachers' group be the one to complete the group of experts or would it be administrators with the teachers?

Because it has now become eminently clear to parents that they have very little control over the education of their children, my question is this: Do you really expect the American people to accept that it is really just a struggle between two groups of experts and thus they have very little control over the education of their children? Do you expect us to really accept it? Second, as an educator, would you *want* us to accept the current situation in which we have almost no control over the education of our children? In effect, we are being told that we needn't be concerned about that. We don't have to be responsible because we have turned it over to experts. But can you really expect parents to be responsible if you present to us a system of governance that says, "Be content with the fact that our education is no longer controlled by you but by a group of experts?"

John Dunlop (National Education Association): If the public wants its will to be exerted beyond what it is now in educational policy making, all mechanisms for that are in place right now. I don't think you have to go into the collective bargaining process.

David Seeley: This conference is concerned with that aspect of the educational governance process that is now being done at the bargaining table, which is what we now call the fourth branch of the government. All we are saying is "O.K., there are certain parts of these decisions that are being removed from the public arena. It is very hard to get at them."

John Dunlop: They were never there in the first place.

David Seeley: But you will find that the board says, "We can't discuss this. It's in negotiations." Or, "This is an issue that has already been settled. You are concerned about how we are allocating money we should be held accountable for, but that was already decided in negotiations. These are mandated costs. You can't do anything about them." That's what we are trying to crack.

John Dunlop: I think the mechanisms are all there for cracking it. What I heard from the Rochester experience is that they felt more comfortable with Gayle as their representative than the representative they already elected because Gayle was basically credible, and all those other people were not. It says something not only about those people who are managers and administrators, but it also says something about the electorate. I think that is crucial. I don't think American education was conceived and operated on the principle of some giant conspiracy on the part of experts. The American public deferred to experts. I would be willing to bet that if you were to poll the mass of the public in America—this is only visceral—and ask them how they want their representative to act on school boards, at the delegate end of the spectrum or the trustee end of the spectrum, they would come out for the trustee end of the spectrum. Some of the problems that are faced in American education are fundamental to the operation of our society. Desegregation, textbook selection, and the Charleston, West Virginia, controversy over the religious content of the curriculum go right to the heart of some problems in American society that are not capable of easy solution, and I think that there is a mass of public out there that is willing to defer to the trustee.

David Seeley: I agree with you. I think most people would vote for the trustee model. What surprises me is that I would think teacher representatives would be trying to promote a more democratic process, because I predict what you will find is that the public will vote for the trustee model but that when they become dissatisfied— they are increasingly getting dissatisfied with what the trustees are doing—they will vote with their feet. They will vote for the voucher thing in California if the professional educators' unions and administrators keep going the way they are. That's how they will treat the trustee situation. I would think if you want to preserve public education you would be fighting to promote a more democratic process so that the public would feel they have some stake in this thing and cannot afford to turn it over to a bunch of people with whom they are increasingly losing contact.

John Dunlop: My answer, David, is that all the mechanisms are there.

David Seeley: And you should be fighting with us to make them work.

Happy Fernandez (Parents' Union for Public Schools in Philadelphia): John, could you clarify how far you are willing to open up and allow citizens, if not representation at the table, information about the collective bargaining process?

John Dunlop: My experience in twelve years of bargaining is that we have never been capable of controlling what the other side says in collective bargaining. And we strenuously resist them controlling what we say in collective bargaining. If the school board desires to inform parents or citizens of what has transpired in bargaining, that's their prerogative, just as it is our prerogative to inform our own teachers of what is going on in bargaining. It seems to me the problem is getting the citizens to tell the representative what to do. I don't think you are doing that.

Happy Fernandez: That's where I'm puzzled. Why doesn't the union give out information and meet with the parents?

John Dunlop: They are not our constituency.

Happy Fernandez: Parents are not going to get the full picture by just talking with the board side. We want to talk with the union side to hear firsthand what your position is, not through the AFT newsletters. We'd like to meet union people personally to hear what their side is; we don't trust the board. How can you deal with a situation if you don't know all the facts?

John Dunlop: My answer is elect officials you have confidence in.

Happy Fernandez: But until that happens, we still have to live, our kids still attend schools, and we still have to survive in our city.

Kurt Hanslowe (Cornell University): A quick factual point: if anyone was a master of fishbowl bargaining, it was Walter Reuther. Goldfish bowl bargaining was one of his favorite ploys. He liked nothing better than talking to the public, and he played the public in a masterful way that would frustrate the auto industry. For you to say just "you are not part of my constituency" is not a satisfactory answer to Ms. Hernandez. I don't share the view that they are not part of the constituency.

Edward Krinsky (Wisconsin Center for Public Policy): The citizen participants are not doing their job of citizen participation and electing their representatives to represent them. I sense that people are talking at each other or across each other and not focusing on the problem. The unions are not going to be convinced—and I don't blame them a bit—that sunshine bargaining is an answer to anything, and they are not going to agree that citizens or other third-party groups belong at the bargaining table. Citizen groups are not going to believe that they have no place and no right to have greater access—I don't blame them a bit. I think that the focus should be very narrow. These positions can be maintained: you can have collective bargaining, greater democracy, greater citizen rights, and you can have them without sunshine bargaining. I hope this conference will focus on how you achieve that.

David Seeley: I hope there may be a followup to this conference, in which we say, "O.K., we've arrived at a framework," and we list a lot of other things—prebargaining, factfinding, perhaps enforcing the rule of completing your bargaining before the budget is adopted, which the Taylor Law supposedly requires but nobody ever pays attention to—possibly the technique of the citizen committee as in Berkeley or the parent representative as in Rochester, the community school board representation as in New York. There are a lot of techniques that we have mentioned that haven't seriously been discussed, except maybe "sunshine."

But there is one aspect that doesn't even fall in this discussion, and that has to do with the delegation of experts. We all really want to defer to experts at times. Experts have something to offer us. My observation, in New York at least, is that for consulting with experts and getting their best thinking on how to run an educational system, the collective bargaining session is a terrible place to do it. It is not a bad place to say how much money you want. But when it comes to issues like what is the best way of assigning staff at the school level to deal with student discipline, it doesn't work. It doesn't work to have these issues come into a session going on at three a.m. in the Plaza, with the mayor jumping in saying "I don't have the money to give you, but why don't you take all this other stuff, that doesn't cost us anything?" That's not only bad from the public's point of view, but I would think wouldn't be very satisfactory from the professionals' point of view. Are you really getting consultation with the best thinking in this school system? I think Krinsky is right. Wouldn't it be better for all of us to find some way to at least discuss some of these issues within a framework where we can exchange ideas and maybe invent better ways of doing it? We are all missing the boat here on some of these knotty problems. You might experiment with us on alternative ways of taking them out of pressure-cooker collective bargaining and putting them into some kind of joint committees.

John Dunlop: That's where we are going to part company. I really believe in collective bargaining. I think it can be a calm process for very rational discourse. Whatever warps intrude into it by either party are on a personality basis, and they are going to occur no matter what kind of forum you are in. I don't see every bargaining situation generating a so-called pressure cooker where everything is bought through the deferring of payment of money. That just doesn't happen, not in the vast majority of bargaining that I've been involved in.

Kurt Hanslowe: I think that the reason that we have tended to focus on the collective bargaining process is because there are some very serious conflicts between the collective bargaining process and the running of government in the way to which we were accustomed. Those tensions keep moving us to the process. I also am inclined to agree that one should shift the focus, accepting those tensions, to how you cope with the process, how you contain the process, how you integrate the process of collective bargaining with public administration—without that, those states that have not seen fit to pass bargaining laws may well be right.

The other thing is that we are not experiencing this problem of tensions and dissatisfaction in just the area of collective bargaining; we are experiencing it in all fields of public administration. We used to think that our administrative agencies were supposed to represent the public interest, so when we suspect that those administrative agencies tend to be in cahoots with those they are supposed to regulate, we try to figure out different ways of getting the public interest articulated. We tend to suspect that those school boards which Mr. Dunlop is so fond of have a tendency, once collective bargaining arises, to be in cahoots with the teachers' organizations; and we want to figure out ways of containing the process. You may shout at each other, but basically you are in cahoots with each other. What the rest of us are trying to do is not to eliminate the process but to control it. We are doing this in all kinds of ways that you tend not to like, such as limiting the scope of bargaining and introducing sunshine laws. We are looking at all kinds of means and devices. You better face the fact that although you have a lovely harmonious triangular relationship—union, school board, and neutrals—there are others around who want to get in on the action.

John Dunlop: Do you teach labor law? Then you are part and parcel of the cahoots—cohorts. I don't think you can take a position saying we all have a neat little world. I agree with the fundamental premise that the academics—you included—the unions, and the school boards may have some collusive elements about them. But don't separate yourself from that. You are part and parcel of it.

Kurt Hanslowe: I suppose owning up to what I'm doing is an honest thing. Isn't it?

Donald Magruder (Florida School Boards Association): We have met the enemy and he is us.

VI.

The Parents' Role in Collective Bargaining

Happy Craven Fernandez

Developing independent parent organizations that can bargain for the interests of parents and their children is a prerequisite for any substantive change in the destructive power struggles surrounding collective bargaining in public education. There is increasing evidence that the present collective bargaining process in public education serves only to protect the interests of the two groups who now monopolize the power in public school systems, the teachers' unions and the school officials. Unfortunately, neither group has the students' needs as their primary interest.

My experience as a parent in the Philadelphia school system and information gathered from other school districts around the country have given me evidence that the teachers' unions have become a dominant political and economic force able to formulate educational policy and to determine the allocation of scarce resources. The teachers' unions certainly outmuscle parent groups and taxpayer associations because of their strong organizational base and because of the laws governing collective bargaining for public employees. It has been parents' experience that because of the heat generated at the bargaining table and because of the distance and barriers between school board members and the parents and students, school officials tend to lose sight of public concerns, especially student concerns, at the bargaining table.[1] Independent parent organizations are needed to be advocates for the children. Parents' one vested interest is to see that their children get a quality education.

---

1. By *school officials,* I mean both school board members and school administrators. See distinctions between these roles made on pp. 88–89.

Conflicting Interests of School Officials

At its heart, the collective bargaining process, which has been adopted almost wholesale from the private sector collective bargaining model, is the way for teachers as employees to negotiate salary scales and working conditions. It is not an effective model or even the proper arena to negotiate for educational quality for students.

In theory, the school board should be primarily concerned with providing a quality education for students. In practice, the school boards represent the diverse interests of adults who hold power in the community: the political machines, the economic establishment, the religious institutions, and often the ethnic and fraternal societies. Whether elected or appointed, the school boards are composed of adults with economic and political power. To maintain their position, school board members strive to please a variety of constituents: politicians, bankers, taxpayers. Most school board members are people with good intentions and deep senses of civic duty. But when it comes time to make difficult choices, they are often caught between competing and conflicting interests. Adults with the clout, political and economic, have much more leverage and influence than students who have no economic power and no vote. Students' interests too often are sacrificed in the heat of negotiations and budget crises. In many school districts, this has caused a severe credibility gap between school officials and the consumers. At a recent community meeting with the negotiators for the Philadelphia school district and the teachers' union, the school district's chief negotiator was greeted with groans and pained laughter when he urged parents and citizens to put their "trust in the school board to use managerial prerogative in the best interests of students."

Another major cause of school boards' failure to consistently represent the interests of students and parents is the consolidation of school districts and the resulting emergence of the administrative bureaucracy. The consolidation of school districts in America from eighty-three thousand in 1950 to seventeen thousand in 1976 has meant a sharp reduction in the numbers of school board members who are known by and accessible to parents, students, and other citizens. In large urban districts, one board member may represent a quarter-million people.

The consolidation has also produced larger school districts and the growth of a layer of administrators hired by the school board to manage the sprawling bureaucracy. These experts wield extensive power and can be another barrier between the school boards and the parents. The administrators sometimes use their professionalism to inhibit parent and citizen participation; they may use jargon and long titles that confuse or intimidate many parents.

School administrators not only manage but, in effect, make policy in school districts. They are frequently able to control information and outmaneuver the volunteer, part-time school board members. A major problem with this shift of power from school boards to school administrators is the tendency of career bureaucrats to perpetuate the system. Serving the system can easily become a higher priority than serving students.

In the years ahead, as the school age population declines and the competition for scarce budget dollars increases in many communities, school boards and administrators will be faced with even more severe budget pressures, which will make it difficult if not impossible for them to be advocates for children, who are so powerless.

Teacher vs. Parent Interests

Teachers' unions are formed as private organizations to represent the interests of teachers (and other employees in some districts). Union leadership is accountable only to its members. In some instances, the interests of teachers and students or parents happen to coincide on issues like smaller class size or fully funded programs. The teachers' union can in these instances be said to benefit students.

But on many issues in contract negotiations, teachers' interests are either not directly related to or are divergent from students and parent interests: some examples are restrictions on the number of evening meetings teachers can be asked to attend; restrictions on the length of the school day, which sometimes result in a race for the door between students and employees; the past practices clause, which has been used to guard the status quo; the transfer and dismissal guidelines, which make it most difficult to weed out incompetent teachers.

In addition, the political power of public sector unions is increasing at a frightening rate, especially when compared to the minuscule resources available to parents and students to lobby for their interests. Teacher organizations (the National Education Association and the American Federation of Teachers) have millions of dollars to spend each year to influence legislation at the federal, state, and local levels.[2]

The solutions to these problems do not lie in excluding teachers from the decision-making process in public education or denying teachers the right to bargain collectively for the terms of their employment. Rather, the decision-making process should be altered to include parents and students as consumers. Also, there need to be limits on the

---

2. Lawrence Pierce, "Teachers' Organizations and Bargaining: Power Imbalance in the Public Sphere," in *Public Testimony on Public Schools* (National Committee for Citizens in Education, 1976), pp. 131, 133.

scope and content of collective bargaining between the employees and school districts so that there are significant areas of policy and practice left to be negotiated between school boards and parents.

The Parents' Role in Bargaining

How can parents alter the power structure that is currently monopolized by the teachers' unions and school officials? How can parents become a third party with power to affect the decisions that determine their children's school experience?

One option would be to undermine the teachers' union, oppose their collective bargaining rights, and place trust and the power in the hands of school boards. I reject this option as unwise and probably impossible.

A second option is to try to become a third party to the contract negotiations between the teachers' union and school district. I reject this option because it contradicts the basic assumption that employees have a right to bargain collectively with their employer on wages and working conditions. It is also not feasible because parent organizations do not at present have the money to pay staff or professional negotiators to attend the endless negotiating sessions and report back directly to all the parents. In addition, the critical compromises would very likely be worked out somewhere other than at the bargaining table.

A third option is to try to influence the negotiating process between the employees and employer by presenting the parents' analysis and perspective on the issues developed by the two sides before, during, and after the negotiations. Many parent groups, including Parents' Union for Public Schools in Philadelphia, are doing this and will continue to do it. A severe limitation of this third option, however, is that parents are in a reactive rather than a proactive position. Parents' only power is persuasion rather than demand backed by law. In addition, many vital educational issues affecting students are not addressed and should not be addressed in bargaining between employer and employee.

A fourth option is to take legal action to limit the scope of collective bargaining between the employees and employer so that bargaining is limited to wages and working conditions, narrowly defined. This would prevent the employee unions from arguing that every area of policy and practice affects working conditions and therefore nothing can be changed without prior negotiation with teacher union representatives. The past practices clause in the Philadelphia Federation of Teachers' contract has this kind of stranglehold on educational policy and practice; for example, it has been used to ban parents from visiting classrooms and to ban individualized report cards.

One legal step related to this fourth option was taken in 1975 by

Parents' Union when it filed suit charging that the board of education had unlawfully delegated educational policy-making authority and responsibility to a nonpublic body, the teachers' organization. Six areas of the 1973 contract between the School District of Philadelphia and the Philadelphia Federation of Teachers were challenged. The case is still pending. The suit addresses the issues of the scope of collective bargaining agreements and the balance between the teachers' collective bargaining rights and the school board responsibility to make policy, but it fails to address the critical issue of the parents' prerogative and parents' rights.

A fifth option is for parent groups to lobby for legislation that would put some contraints on the collective bargaining process in the public sector so that strikes, which deprive the students of their right to an education, are minimized or prevented. For example, binding arbitration is one possibility that needs full exploration.[3] Other techniques that are being discussed and explored are setting strict timetables for the bargaining process, perhaps including mandated contract expiration dates, and the use of state-appointed fact finders and mediators.

The Parents' Contract

The sixth option is for parents to organize into independent parent organizations that can bargain for the interests of their children. A parents' contract negotiated with the school board would define in writing and give the force of law equivalent to a teachers' contract to those policies directly affecting the quality of the student's educational experience, specifically, the rights of parents as advocates for their child's interests. Figure 1 comprises three diagrams that illustrate the changes in the decision-making equation when parents assert a role.

The law already contains some guarantees affecting the quality of the students' education. A new federal law, the Education for All Handicapped Children Act of 1975 (Pub. L. No. 94-142), is designed to guarantee the right of children with handicapping conditions to an educational experience that is individualized and appropriate. Essential to the testing and placement of each child are the due process procedures spelled out in the legislation. Parents and, when possible, the students are parties involved in the process of finding an appropriate educational experience. Parents are there to be the advocates for the student's best interest. They have the right to bring an advocate to the conferences to provide advice and support. Basic decisions about the students cannot be made without the parent's consent.

---

3. See Lawrence Pierce, "Teachers' Organizations and Bargaining: Power Imbalance in the Public Sphere," in *Public Testimony on Public Schools* (National Committee for Citizens in Education, 1976), pp. 145–57.

Figure 1. Effects of Teacher and Parent Contracts on Decision Making

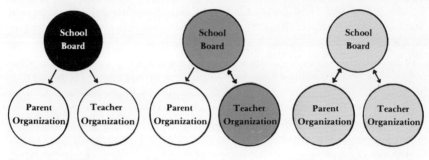

No Contract Obligations.
Power is lodged in the school
board. Teachers and parents
are excluded.

*Teacher–School Board
Contract.*
Power is shared with teach-
ers. Parents are excluded.

*Teacher–School Board/Par-
ent–School Board Contracts.*
Power is shared with parents
and teachers.

This federal legislation provides the strongest basis to date for parental input into the decisions directly affecting their child's daily educational experience. In many school districts, however, the letter and spirit of this law are being implemented very slowly. In Philadelphia, the Parents' Union and the Education Law Center are jointly training parent advocates to help parents negotiate with the system and fully exercise their rights under the law.

The parent's right to be involved in the decision-making process in school has been buttressed by the parent advisory councils established by the Title I federal legislation. Parent advisory councils are required in every school district that receives Title I funds (for "educationally disadvantaged" students in "economically disadvantaged" schools) and have the authority to make input into, review, and sign off on Title I budgets. In some school districts this federal legislation provides an effective lever for parents affected by Title I programs, while in other districts the parent advisory councils are controlled by school officials.

State laws provide another basis for guaranteeing that students receive a quality education. For example, the Pennsylvania constitution states that students should receive a "thorough and efficient" education, and parts of the state school code set mandates for some of the factors undergirding quality education. The state school code requires that students receive 180 days (and 990 hours) of instruction each year—yet in practice even that state law has been eroded by another state law, Public Employee Relations Act (Pub. L. 563, no. 195, 43 P.S.) of 1970, that gives teachers the right to strike.

Several states have legislation that mandates citizen-parent roles in decision making. Florida, for example, has citizen advisory councils mandated for each district; assessment of the effectiveness of the councils is now available.[4] New Jersey also has a new mandate for citizen-parent involvement in development of curricula, establishment of district budgets, and hiring and dismissal of personnel. It is part of the "thorough and efficient" mandate.[5]

Using the present federal and state laws as a beginning, a parents' contract would ideally include other rights and procedural safeguards over the factors directly affecting a child's education. Some parents' rights not yet clearly established by law but essential to a meaningful parents' contract include the parents' right to visit schools and classrooms, their right to a grievance procedure, their right to be involved in devising an appropriate educational plan for their child. These provisions might be similar to those which exist for handicapped children under the new federal law.

The parents' contract should also establish effective mechanisms to inform parents of their rights, their child's progress, and the programs and process of the whole school. The parents' contract would also provide for meaningful parental input into the major determinants of the educational experience of the student: namely, the selection of school staff, especially the principal and teachers; curriculum development; and budget priorities. In school districts where school-level management returns decision-making responsibility on these vital issues to the local school, the parents' contract would guarantee rights of parents; other issues affecting the quality of education would be decided by a local school council consisting of school employees and the consumers.

Need for Independent Parent Organizations

In order for parents to be able to influence the bargaining, take legal action to limit the content of bargaining, lobby to secure constraints on the process of bargaining, or negotiate for a parents' contract, they need to form independent parents' organizations in each school district and, ideally, at each school within the district.

Parent organizations that are controlled or financed by school officials can easily be pressured or coopted by school officials in times of crisis, especially in those controversies concerning collective bargaining issues. It is probably more common for parent organizations that are controlled by school officials to be kept in a servant role, raising funds and doing petty tasks. As a result, members lack the energy and

---

4. This report may be obtained from the Institute for Responsive Education, 704 Commonwealth Avenue, Boston, Massachusetts 02215.

5. More information is available from the Commissioner of Education, State of New Jersey, State Street, Trenton, New Jersey 08601.

experience to deal with substantive issues like budgets, contracts, or selection of personnel. Many parents who want a parent organization that deals with the basic issues become frustrated and bored and drop out of the controlled parent associations.

As independent parent organizations continue to develop in communities around the country, they can devise ways to meaningfully exercise influence over bargaining agreements and implement parent contracts. This, in turn, will foster the development of new independent parent groups as more parents realize it is possible to play a meaningful role in shaping the experience their children have in the public schools.

In another age, Lord Acton made his famous pronouncement "Power corrupts and absolute power corrupts absolutely." The destructive power struggles between the teachers' unions and school officials are making the truth of that statement increasingly apparent and painfully immediate to students today. My own three children have been asking since school was out in June, "Mom, do you think there will be school in September?" We are facing the prospect of another strike. For my eleven-year-old son, it will be the third such September in six years of school.

Independent parent organizations that can gain power and exercise it on behalf of children are one way to alter the present power balance; decisions are made more justly and wisely if they include all parties who are affected by the consequences of the decisions. But, as Frederick Douglass noted, "Power never concedes anything without a struggle, it never has and never will." Developing independent parent organizations that serve as advocates for school children will be a long struggle. It will take a long time both to develop the organizations and to win the legal rights that will guarantee a parental role in decision making in public education. Parents cannot assume that those in power will readily hand over any significant areas of decision making. Parents will have to find ways to assert and expand their rights and role.

Parents, who have a lifelong responsibility for their children, are an essential group to be fully involved in decisions affecting schools. Parents who are involved in decisions that affect them and their children will be among the most loyal and committed to public education. Allowing them to participate makes administration of the schools much more cumbersome and time-consuming, like most democratic processes. It may be very threatening to those who are accustomed to exercising absolute power absolutely. But meaningful involvement of parents in decisions affecting public schools is a must. Meaningful involvement of the consumer of publicly supported services may well be our major historical achievement in the last decades of the twentieth century.

Response

Comment by Edward B. Krinsky

The role of parents in collective bargaining in public education is an important topic and one that is in need of clarification and analysis. It involves questions about how parents and other public groups can make their influence felt on an essentially bilateral collective bargaining process. There is skepticism about who, if anyone, represents the interests of these public groups. Teacher unions do not claim to represent the public, nor should they. School boards are governmental structures that are supposed to be representative, but on any given issue there may be reason to question whether this is so.

I awaited receipt of Ms. Fernandez's paper with some anxiety since I was not familiar with either Ms. Fernandez or the Parents' Union for Public Schools in Philadelphia. I feared that the paper would be both antagonistic to collective bargaining per se and unrealistic in the suggestions for what to do about the situation. This fear was based on numerous experiences which I have had in which various groups purporting to represent the public have advocated increased public participation in the bargaining process without understanding or accepting the appropriate role of unions and collective bargaining. I am pleased to say that Ms. Fernandez's paper does not fit such a stereotype and that it is, in fact, a sound paper that recognizes the importance of collective bargaining, although not without pointing out some of its shortcomings, and makes reasoned suggestions for improving the situation. I find myself in agreement with many of the options which she presents.

It is my view, in agreement with Ms. Fernandez, that the only way parents and other "publics" will be heard is if they organize and thus become a force to be reckoned with. If parent groups can be ignored, they need to be better organized. They have to be able to impose a political or economic cost when they are not listened to, and they have to be able to demonstrate to decision makers that there are benefits to be had from listening to them.

Ms. Fernandez is correct when she indicates that the focus of the efforts of parent groups for change should be on the school board and school administration. Teachers' unions do not have a legal mandate to represent anyone other than those in the bargaining unit. They may in fact share the views of parent groups on some issues, but they will put their constituents' interests first. The school board, on the other hand, is supposed to represent the public, whether or not it in fact does so, but the interests of parents will be lost or diluted in school board decisions unless there is a strong, clear, well-organized group demanding that its views be considered.

There are, of course, great difficulties in creating and maintaining a strong parent group. One important difficulty, which I am sure Ms. Fernandez knows much more about than I do, is that one cannot easily talk about "the view of parents" since there are often as many views as there are parents. Parents are also citizens, and while they may want educational quality for their children, what they mean by educational quality and what they are willing to sacrifice to get it may depend on myriad factors: economic status, educational level, cultural heritage, allegiance to public education, number and ages of their children in the school system, or what school their children attend. In fact, the diversity of parent views poses a danger for organized parent groups. School board members and school administrators may discount the representativeness of any parent group that presents itself and may use that argument to ignore the group's recommendations. There may be similar problems when one attempts to identify the interests of students, the other group with which Ms. Fernandez is concerned.

I am willing to assume, however, for argument's sake that strongly organized, representative groups of parents (and perhaps students) can come into being and surmount such critical problems as finances and staffing, however difficult that may be. Once that very large hurdle is overcome, then I agree with Ms. Fernandez that the key questions involve how such groups can influence the decision making.

The notion that teacher unions have become too strong is an underlying theme in Ms. Fernandez's paper. I am not going to debate that. Surely there are such examples, but there are countless examples where teacher unions are not strong at all. Where they are strong, they have organized well, have the full support of teachers, and have learned to bargain and to exercise their organizational skills to influence the school board and other influential segments of the community; that is, as organizations, they have done just what Ms. Fernandez would like parent organizations to do. If teacher unions have become somewhat too powerful, it is no doubt partly because there have not been well-organized countervailing interest groups to balance the equation. The typical school board is not going to be able to represent the public interest, however it is defined, unless that interest is well articulated and organized when crisis decisions have to be made. Ms. Fernandez is right in saying that most school board members mean well and try hard, but she is also right that she cannot depend on school board members to represent her. So she wants to organize to see to it that they do.

Ms. Fernandez rightly rejects the option of working to oppose collective bargaining. That would serve to take away important employee rights and would also drive a wedge between unionized employees and parents, something which I do not believe would result in greater influence for parents. Whether or not parents always like what is negotiated, it is a fact that unions are a check on unilateral action by the school board, and parent groups might derive benefits from alliance with groups that can influence the school board.

In my view, Ms. Fernandez also is correct when she rejects the option of giving parent groups a seat at the bargaining table. Collective bargaining over wages, hours, and conditions of employment should be between employee unions and the employer or the representative of the employer. School employees are not hired by parents or students. The presence of such additional groups would add immensely to the complexity of reaching peaceful agreements in a timely manner. Also, if parents and students come to the bargaining table, why not taxpayer groups and neighborhood associations? The result of insistence on the inclusion of additional parties to the bargaining would be to increase the chances of disruption of services, when it is minimization of such disruption that a parent group would seek to achieve.

Ms. Fernandez's third option is a viable one in my view. That is, well-organized parent groups can and should present their perspective on the issues being bargained; they should present their views to both sides but particularly to the school board. If there is a statute, such as the California or the new Wisconsin statute, that requires the parties to make public their initial bargaining demands, an organized parent group could easily address the specific issues being considered by the bargainers. School boards might be encouraged (or required by law) to provide an opportunity for public reaction to initial bargaining positions of the school board and the union. I stress *initial* bargaining positions because the boundaries of the bargain would be known, but there would not be interference with the bargaining once it began. The public should know what subjects are being bargained so that public groups and individuals can communicate their views to the bargainers in a timely way. I do not advocate that the bargaining process itself be open to the public.

I have no opinion about the fourth option proposed by Ms.

Fernandez. If the law defines the scope of bargaining and it is adminis-
tered by a competent and neutral labor relations agency, there should be
no need for lawsuits by parent groups. It is certainly appropriate,
however, for parent groups to remain vigilant to the possibility that the
particular school board will abdicate its legal responsibilities and
bargain on subjects that it should not in order to maintain peaceful
relationships with the union. Vigilance is also advisable because unions
will not necessarily let scope-of-bargaining decisions by labor agencies
dictate the scope of their bargaining demands; they will demand
whatever they view as in the best interests of their constituents.

The fifth option spelled out by Ms. Fernandez is a sensible one. It is
my view that any group that wants to exert influence over the rules of
the game is well advised to have a lobbyist. However unfortunate, it is
the case that laws are generally compromises reached among competing
interest groups. If parents are a separate interest, they should be in there
lobbying. As mentioned earlier, however, there may be a problem in
persuading legislators that a particular group speaks for parents in
general. Here, one tangential but important point is worthy of mention.
One reason given by Ms. Fernandez for having a parent lobby is to
explore alternatives to the strike and, in particular, binding arbitration.
This presents a dilemma to any advocate of greater local representation:
strikes will be reduced by having arbitration, but arbitration reduces or
eliminates the influence of the community since an arbitrator makes a
decision binding on everyone and the arbitrator generally is not politically responsible to anyone in the jurisdiction in which he or she is
operating.

The concept of Ms. Fernandez's option six of having parent groups
make contractual agreements with the school board seems unobjection-
able, although I cannot clearly visualize the substance of such arrange-
ments. I would be interested in hearing more about parent contracts and
what subjects they could encompass without infringing upon the legal
obligations of the school board or depriving unions of their statutory
collective bargaining rights; Ms. Fernandez mentions as possible examples increased parent visits to schools and classrooms and involvement
in educational planning. Such a contract would have to be compatible
with the teacher contract. Also, if these agreements involve longer hours
and greater obligations for teachers, they will also involve additional
expense because the unions will insist on pay for these activities. In
making their demands, parent groups may have to weigh carefully the
costs they impose measured against the resulting benefits.

In their drive for influence parent groups should not write off
unions of teachers and other school employees. There is no reason why
parent groups and teacher unions need to be on opposite sides of all

issues. If they can identify areas of mutual concern for students, they may be able to devise strategies for using their collective influence to accomplish joint goals. Parents may strongly object to the disruption of their children's education by teacher strikes, but they may reap great benefits if the influence of unions can be brought to bear in a constructive way to improve the status of students and parents in school affairs. Thus, on selected issues, a parent union could work in a coalition with an employee's union to influence the school board, while on other issues the parent union might be more allied with the school board position.

In conclusion, I think that Ms. Fernandez is on the right track. She is also correct that change will not come easily. She has to face the same question that every union and movement has to face, how to build a strong and effective organization and how to keep it that way. How does one sustain a parent interest group, and how does the organization have the means, financial and otherwise, to make its influence felt over a long period of time?

Discussion Highlights

Throughout the conference, "access" advocates had stressed that increased information about the content of negotiations was essential to a citizen's ability to positively influence public education, while the labor professionals defended the need for confidentiality during negotiations. A second major topic of controversy had been the problem of how to identify legitimate representatives of the public. Drawing on both topics in the final session, David Seeley subordinated the problem of legitimacy of representation to the problem of restriction of information and its tendency to frustrate democratic determination of public policy—*Editor*.

David Seeley (Public Education Association): To go back a little and address the question of who is the public, let me spell out more of what it is we are trying to achieve. I'll give an example. In 1975, you may recall, we had a financial crisis. Everything was frozen, not just wages but everything. The teacher contract was the first collective bargaining negotiation to start after the crisis and the freeze were announced in June. The mayor got on the tube and said, "Hey, we're in trouble," and the teachers were just beginning negotiations for a contract that was going to run out on September 9. I don't want to get into the substance of this dispute, but I want to tell you the procedural situation because nobody could disagree that there was an extremely important public policy question about the use of scarce resources in the city. There was a clear public policy choice. With the available money, are you going to retain people on the job or are you going to give increases? We, obviously, took the position that we should retain the people on the job; the union took the position that they would rather have the increases, which is as I understand it a classic union position. And they did end up winning longevity increases of various kinds (about $100 million). The important thing is that there was absolutely no debate within New York City about the relative merits of either option. No public discussion, no editorial discussion about it. There was no editorial discussion because the media did not report that there were any such options.

I could see it happening. PEA—this citizens' group, officious intermeddlers—had done some studies of the budget. We foresaw ten thousand teachers being laid off over the summer, and we could predict enormous disruption to the school system when school opened. There would be incredible dislocation, breach of relationships between teachers and kids, not because of a strike but because of the loss of teachers. We tried to persuade the mediator that this should be reported, and here is what happened: I spoke to one reporter from a major newspaper who said, "Al Shanker insists that they are not asking for any increases in negotiations." And I said, "Why are you believing Al Shanker? He is one of the most skillful, terrific manipulators of the press anybody has ever seen." He said, "O.K. I'll go to the school board." He went to the school board and got the same answers. An interviewer on the radio asked the teacher negotiators if there were any increases in the situation, and they said, "No, we are not talking about increases in this negotiation." This was when it was moving toward a strike or even in the strike. And I called up that interviewer, and I said, "Would you please ask that question of the chief negotiator for the board?" He did, and the president of the school board said the same thing. There was no debate.

I think that the Harold Newmans of the world and the Bob Dohertys and everybody who is concerned about any kind of democratic process ought to be concerned about that decision. There was no public debate. That is my answer to your question about who is the public.